WILDERNESS
SKILLS FOR
WOMEN

marian jordan

WILDERNESS
SKILLS FOR
WOMEN

how to survive heartbreak and other
full-blown meltdowns

B&H
PUBLISHING GROUP

Nashville, Tennessee

08 09 10 11 12   11 10 9 8 7 6 5 4 3 2

Mom and Dad:

Thank you for modeling an unwavering faith in God.

Contents

Acknowledgments

I am forever grateful to the many people who gave of their time, talents, and prayers in support of *Wilderness Skills for Women*. To my dear friends who loved me through my wilderness: Tonya, Anita, Angel, Toni, Lacey, Susannah, Leigh, Muriel, Manonne, and Leti—thank you for speaking God's truth to my heart and for always pointing me back to Jesus. To Catherine King: thank you for editing the manuscript and for always encouraging me through this journey.

A special thank-you to the board of *Redeemed Girl Ministries* (Matt and Jessica, Leti and Chaz, Jason and Susannah, Marc and Leigh, Ryan and Kim, and Jeff and Jenny). Your wisdom and support are priceless!

To the amazing women who allowed me to share their stories: Cristy, Catherine, Sarah, Amy, and Becky. Thank you, not only for your story but for your example. Each of you walked through your wilderness in a way that inspired me and I know will encourage others.

To the wonderful team at B&H Publishing: I'm so blessed to work with individuals who passionately love Jesus and who desire for women to know Him.

I want to thank my family. I love you guys. Mom and Dad, thank you for reminding me that "God is not taking Maalox over my situation" and for your example of faithfulness.

Finally, to my Jesus—You are my Rock, Redeemer, and Refuge. I praise You, for Your promises are true and You are faithful!

introduction

The Full-Blown Meltdown

I don't cry easily.

I'm not a girl who is moved to tears by sappy commercials or movies (except for the film *Stepmom* with Julia Roberts—wow, did I bawl during that one). I'm even unaffected by most of Oprah's programs and *Extreme Home Makeover*. I'm not saying I'm heartless, just not prone to weeping. But when I do cry, girls, let me just say that I AM THE UGLIEST CRIER IN THE ENTIRE WORLD! I've often thought there should be some kind of award for this. Perhaps *People* magazine could run a special issue. Instead of the *50 Most Beautiful People*, they could publish, I don't know, let's say . . . the *50 Most Hideous Criers*. I'm sure I'd rank in the top five.

For starters, I don't do simple tears.

You know, the dainty little single teardrop that flows quietly down a cheek? Nope, not this girl. I have two modes: my tears are guttural or they aren't at all. And when a cry is coming on, there is no stopping it. My weeping begins in my stomach and moves up my entire body until it finally reaches my eyes, where water equivalent of the Mississippi River is unleashed.

First, my chest begins to ache, and then my throat tightens, which is followed by the rounding of my shoulders forward into this hunchbacked position that my friend Tonya likes to call "the accordion." It's a lovely scene. And then, my entire upper body begins to shake—uncontrollably. Technically, I think this state is called "heaving sobs." Whatever it is, it isn't attractive. Finally, my face, my entire face, gets in on the action. I'm pressed for the right words here. Contorted? Sure. But disfigured is probably the better description. Like I said, hideous.

I should know that I am quite the ugly crier because I had plenty of experience in this department last year. Just as a meteorologist can calculate rainfall percentages, likewise, I estimate my tear-fall in a six-month period last year reached a historic high for my entire life. Seriously, I had no idea my body could produce such an impressive volume of saline liquid.

So, why the waterworks? I believe, in nautical terms, this season of my life would be called the perfect storm:

> Heartbreak
>
> Rejection
>
> Humiliation
>
> Disappointment
>
> Unmet desire
>
> Loneliness
>
> Despair

But friends, I simply like to call this season *the wilderness*.

Writing a book entitled *Wilderness Skills for Women* is the result of having lived it. I'll share more of my own story as well as tales of other women who've walked through the wilderness in the upcoming chapters, but until then I want to talk about the "what" and the "why" of the wilderness.

Throughout the Bible, a wilderness season is a time of testing, trying, and training an individual. It is often marked by a period of isolation, loneliness, temptation, sorrow, and waiting. Why? Circumstances that try us, train us. Situations that break us, shape us. Such is the wilderness. In the midst of the "dark night of the soul," we are often miserable, but there, we are made. Transformed by the testing . . . *if* we pass the test, that is.

After weeks of living in the wilderness, something clicked. I realized if a wilderness is supposed to be a test, then I was failing. I was miserably failing to live out the faith I so readily professed.

The click occurred the day a friend offered me some "prescriptive happiness." The breaking point, as I like to refer to it, occurred one afternoon as I lay on my bed in a FBMD. Translation: Full-Blown Meltdown. Girls, you know you've been there! Emotions are spiraling into what I love to call the "crazy place," and the tears, oh the tears, they are full-on.

So, I was in a FBMD when my friend walked into my bedroom one afternoon, saw the mess I was in, and in the desperation of the moment offered me some happy pills. I thought, *Drugs? Me? I'm not clinical or chemical; there isn't a medical reason for this. I'm just having a really bad week. OK . . . six weeks. Make that nine.* When she made the offer, I burst into even more tears, and I saw, perhaps for the first time, what an emotional wreck I'd allowed myself to become.

Seeing myself through her eyes, I saw a girl who didn't seem to have joy. A woman who didn't have assurance that the future was filled with hope, and, therefore, she was living in the pit of despair. I saw a pathetic, broken-down, miserably sad woman who obviously didn't believe that God was in control or had a purpose in her heartbreak.

But I *did* believe—with all of my heart, by the way. I just wasn't choosing to live out what I believed; therefore, my emotions were ruling the day, and I was in the crazy place more often than I care to admit. And do you want to know the worst part? The real tragedy was my witness. My fretful and fearful response to my situation was speaking volumes to a watching world about my faith in my God.

Click.

This is a test.

Click.

I think I'm in danger of flunking this one!

My future joy and happiness lay either in the hands of a pharmaceutical company or the Lord God Almighty. Right then and there, I jumped out of bed, went to my bathroom, washed my face, and took a long hard look at myself. Staring at the broken reflection of myself in the mirror, I realized I needed to start walking by faith. Or rather, to start practicing what I preach.

Oh. Yes, by the way, I think I failed to mention one minor-yet-crucial detail. The miserable, crying, pitiful girl, who was curled up in the fetal position in the FBMD, was none other than yours truly, the Bible teacher. That's right, I soooooooooo love confessing this nugget. I was the one who week in and week out taught others the Word of God and encouraged them to place their hope in God, to believe God for the impossible, and to trust God when life is difficult. I was *that* girl. That was my profession, for goodness sake, and there I was suffering senselessly from my own unbelief.

That day, the breaking point, I cried out to God. I didn't want to live in despair anymore. *Help me! I want joy again. Help me, Lord! I want peace again. Show me why I am an emotional basket case. Where am I failing to live out my faith?*

So, what's a girl to do when she's failing a test? Duh . . . study! Everything I needed to overcome the depression, fear, anxiety, and flat-out misery that I was feeling was at my disposal. I only had to make the decision to apply the truth of God's Word to my circumstances and walk by faith. I don't say this flippantly. No, it wasn't a piece of cake to change my thinking and, therefore, reign in uncontrolled emotions. But I knew I had a decision to make. You see, walking by faith is a choice. I had to choose to believe who my God is, to believe what my God has said, and to believe what my God is able to do.

Turning to the Bible, God taught me how other wilderness wanderers like me came forth triumphant from their seasons of testing in the wilderness. And He also taught me skills that I needed to learn from their experiences. These lessons are what you hold in your hands today. A real survival guide given to me in my most desperate time of need. It is my joy to pass these skills on to women who happen to find themselves lost in the wilderness.

wil·der·ness

\ 'wil-der-nes \ *noun*

1 a (1) : a tract or region uncultivated and uninhabited by human beings (2) : an area essentially undisturbed by human activity together with its naturally developed life community **b** : an empty or pathless area or region . . . **c** : a part of a garden devoted to wild growth . . . **3 a** : a confusing multitude or mass : an indefinitely great number or quantity . . . **b** : a bewildering situation

skill

\ 'skil \ *noun*

2 a : the ability to use one's knowledge effectively and readily in execution or performance **b** : dexterity or coordination especially in the execution of learned physical tasks **3** : a learned power of doing something competently : a developed aptitude or ability <language skills>

—*Merriam-Webster's Collegiate Dictionary Eleventh Edition*

part 1

chapter 1

Welcome to the Wilderness

Jesus was taken into the wild by the Spirit for the Test.
MATTHEW 4:1 (MSG)

One date. Just one itsy-bitsy date (and I'm not referring to the fruit). You know that thing when the guy picks up the girl and takes her out to dinner; that's the kind of date I'm talking about. That's all I wanted—or, rather, thought I needed.

So, I prayed. For a date that is. Not intense, on-my-face type of prayer, but we (God and I) did discuss my need/want of a date on a somewhat regular basis.

A Dating Desert

I truly believed that producing a date wasn't a huge task for the Creator of all life. *Surely*, I surmised, *this wasn't a big deal for God*. Or so my line of reasoning believed, and I had the theology to back it up. *If God is really the all-powerful Creator of the universe, then it would seem that conjuring up one eligible male prospect wouldn't be all that difficult.*

After all, God did speak the world into existence, right?

He does own everything, right?

He does sustain the universe by His awesome power, right?

So how hard could it be for Him to produce one eligible member of the opposite sex? Not too difficult, I would assume. It's not like I'm asking for world peace . . . just dinner.

Yet for nine whole months I didn't even meet one guy that I would have coffee with, much less a full meal. This was a dating desert with no oasis in sight.

So, why did I need a date, you ask? Pride.

I'm not ashamed to admit it. Plain, simple, run-of-the-mill, rhymes-with-tide kind of pride. I guess you could say I wanted to save some face. I, too, wanted to walk away from my last relationship and act like nothing ever happened. It wasn't fair. I, too, wanted someone else to numb the ache . . . to fill the void. I so badly wanted to escape the pain of a breakup with the ease of meeting someone new. I really thought a new guy was the solution to my problem.

But I didn't get to escape the pain so easily. I was alone and facing yet another wedding season, class reunion, baby showers, and summer of family picnics—solo. Like I said, it didn't seem fair; I wanted to have someone as my "plus one" for these can't-go-alone events.

But I didn't.

Since the breakup (or what my friends now refer to as "the incident"), my ex-boyfriend successfully met, dated, got engaged to, and married someone else in the span of the eight short months since we said good-bye. (It is truly mind-blowing the speed at which some people are able to move on.) Yet, there I was, still trying to eat normal food again while he was picking out a groom's cake. What's up with that?

I'll be honest. Perhaps I viewed moving on like a competition. And if that's the case, then he was winning gold in the Olympics, and I was auditioning for the middle school track-and-field team. It just didn't seem fair.

As you can see, my pride desperately needed a date.

But it didn't get one. . . . No escape hatch.

The Breakup

Here's the thing: I *thought* my ex was "the one." I thought I was in *love.* Cupid hit me square between the eyes before I had time to duck. It seemed like this relationship dropped in my life out of nowhere, and after some initial resistance on my part, I finally let go, taking a free fall into my worst fear—being close enough to someone that he could actually hurt me. And guess what, he did.

Bad.

It wasn't his fault, really. Clearly, God had different paths for us. I know this to be true today, and I rejoice. In retrospect, I can say with full conviction that although we were part of one another's journeys only for a season, it was for a grand purpose. But back then, in the midst of long walks and laughing till our sides ached, my silly heart didn't get that memo. My heart didn't know it wasn't for keeps . . . so my heart went for it. It plunged.

I'm the type of girl who throws herself 125 percent into something. Lukewarm is not in my vocabulary. Full throttle. Hold nothing back. Give it all. And I did. I gave my heart.

I'm not ashamed to admit that I loved. I never want to be the girl with a calloused heart who can let go at the drop of a hat. I'm not wired that way. I'm not sure any of us are really. Hardness of heart and ease of separation are the by-products of a broken world where love doesn't last. Love was meant to last. We are supposed to hurt and crumble when our hearts are broken. It seems to me, if we get jaded and stop hurting, we are somehow less human. If my heart didn't break, it means I didn't love. And I *did* love. So when the relationship ended, I was whacked by the pendulum of emotions that flooded my way. I've never experienced a physical pain that compares to the emotional pain I felt.

I remember thinking, *Is there an elephant sitting on my chest? Am I having a heart attack? So, this is why they call it "heartbreak."*

Brutal.

Raw.

I was hemorrhaging with the type of gut-wrenching pain that sears every fiber of your being.

The Grieving Process

The funny/sad thing is they don't let you take sick leave for heartbreak. They really should, you know. I think I will petition Congress for this. Seriously, if people can take off work for the sundry things that we see medical doctors for, we should at least get a few "grieving days." I didn't get my grief time. No, I had to step back into my life, put on my game face, and choke back the emotions—all the while realizing how pathetically true country music lyrics can be at times.

But I did grieve—all five stages.

Allow me to explain. Psychologists suggest there are five stages to the grieving process. And they are:

1. Denial. (I really liked this stage. The phrase "reality bites" takes on a whole new meaning when you leave the denial stage.)

2. Anger. (I'm very thankful that God's grace cleanses even our sinful thoughts!)

3. Bargaining. (I did do quite a bit of shopping, but I don't think that is what is meant by this stage. Bargaining is when a person tries to play "let's make a deal" with God. If you will do this for me, then I will do this for you.)

4. Depression. (Sorry, I can't be funny here.)

5. And finally, Acceptance—sweet Acceptance.

Walking through this multilevel season of grief, filled with its doubts and fears, was for me a journey . . . a harsh wilderness trek through some rough woods and rugged terrain. Often, I felt completely lost in this wilderness. The underbrush of emotions and the steep cliffs of fear surrounded me at every turn. Confused, wounded, scared—and yes, at times, so very lonely.

And then, there were the questions:

How did I get here?

When will I get through a day without crying?

God, is this really part of the plan?

Along the way, there were times I was severely tempted to throw away my camping gear and build a permanent settlement. *Denial is a cozy place to live . . . maybe I'll stay here,* I mused.

Or better yet, *anger sure feels good. Perhaps I'll forward my mail.* Then there's depression. *At least a girl can catch up on her sleep in Depressionville.* But I didn't stay for long at any of these camp-sites . . . although each sure seemed alluring at times. I pressed on through the wilderness, sensing something or Someone was beckoning me forward . . . deeper through the thick darkness . . . toward a glimmer, a spark, a distant Light.

Meanwhile, as I trudged through my own personal wilderness, I had to continue my normal life back in the city. You know, real-world stuff like going to work and attempting to be productive; pulling it together long enough to pretend to be social at dinner parties; smiling my way through other people's weddings; staring blankly at my professors as I tried to concentrate in graduate school; and numbly attending to the everyday tasks of grocery shopping, bill paying, and the dread of every single female—car maintenance. I had stuff to do. So, I had to get out of bed and get on with life.

On those occasions when I did venture back into the real world, amidst the whole and happy people, I heard every relationship cliché under the sun from well-meaning friends, family, and the occasional stranger who could see my pain from a mile away. Great truths like:

"God has someone better for you." (Oh, really? And you know this because . . . ?)

"This will all be used for good one day, you'll see."

"Sometimes 'good' is the enemy of God's 'best.'"

"Mr. Right is just right around the corner." (Aw, shucks.)

"Your heart will not break this badly the next time." (PS: not the greatest words of comfort.)

And my all-time favorite (drumroll please): "At least you don't look as old as you really are."

It amazed me how often well-intentioned people made me cry.

You're probably thinking, *It's just a breakup. Get over it . . . move on.* I did move on. Sure, I had to go through the grief process of losing my best friend and figuring out who my new "first call" would be. That was the easy part of the wilderness. Honestly, my grief over time wasn't about missing the guy or about not having a boyfriend; it was about something profoundly deeper—I was grieving the death of hope. Sure, it was a misplaced hope, but I will address that problem in another chapter. Until then, understand this: my grief was over the loss of some*one* and some*thing* all at the same time. I mourned, deeply mourned, the death of a desire: the desire to be married.

You see, I'd *hoped* he was "the one." I'd hoped that my dating days had come to an end. I'd hoped that finally I would be the one picking out china and planning a guest list. But when the relationship ended, I was right back where I started two years before, but this time the dance floor wasn't nearly as crowded. Most—slash that—90 percent of my friends were now married and either planning babies or buying car seat number two. I guess you could say I thought it was my turn. But when my relationship ended, not only did I feel hurt and alone; I also felt like the title of best-selling book series *Left Behind.*

The main problem was that I, like most girls I know, let my heart follow my mind. I painted this perfect little picture in my head of what I thought our life together would be like: our home, our friends, our kids, our vacations, our ministry, and, of course, our wedding. I was so busy planning "our future" that I lost track of the issues in "our present." Looking back, I realize I placed the hope of my future security and happiness in this image I conjured up in my mind. And then, one arduous summer night, we came to the conclusion that our futures weren't entwined and different paths lay before us.

Poof . . . it was all gone.

So what was I supposed to do now with all *my* plans? How did I go forward into a future *without* him that I'd already mapped out in my mind *with* him? This wasn't the plan. This certainly wasn't *my* plan. And somewhere in my heart arose anger at the One I knew full and well had a hand in all of this: God Almighty.

Do you remember the second stage of grief? Yep, that's right, it's called anger. And my anger was unleashed at the most unlikely person—the God whom I loved deeply and served with all my heart. You see, I *knew* it was God who said no. My faith was strong enough to understand that the "perfect will of the Lord cannot be thwarted" (Job 42:2 paraphrase). I knew God was the One who closed the door. We both did. Yet, I was so confused; I truly thought I was following God's plan. So if I was following God's will, then why did I feel like an eighteen-wheeler had driven over my heart?

My life quickly moved from a breakup to a battlefield. The fight was on, and this fight was for my faith. An internal Enemy worked overtime in my thought life. The questions were the worst part. I'd lie my head on my pillow at night, desperately trying to fall asleep, and then they would come. The primary question targeted at my heart was sinister: *If God is so good, then why do you hurt so bad?* This question was followed by other tauntings:

How can you trust a God who would purposefully inflict such pain in your life?

How could He—that God you love so much—have allowed this to happen?

I thought Jesus loved you and had a wonderful plan for your life. Does this wonderful plan include public humiliation, rejection, heartbreak, and possibly lifelong singleness?

It seems your God has blessings for everyone but you. You are such a fool. That trust of yours is pathetic. You would be happier if you would just bail on following that Jesus.

Common Ground

Welcome to my most recent wilderness season.

What about yours? Where has life led you that is difficult, disappointing, or defeating? What journey are you traveling that is sending you into meltdown mode?

We all have our tale of heartbreak. Whether it's a breakup, miscarriage, personal failure, illness, financial crisis, infertility, divorce, death, abandonment . . . not one person reading this is immune to a wilderness season. Each woman's wilderness just bears a different name.

I know this much to be true because while I trekked through Brokenheart Bend, I had friends facing some fierce terrain of their own. Down the street a close friend dealt with the heartbreak of multiple miscarriages as she time and again hoped for a child, only to have her hope dashed within weeks of conception. Across town, another girlfriend struggled to put her life back together after watching her precious mother lose a battle with cancer.

The list goes on. While I waited for my heart to heal, another close friend waited and waited for a job offer during a long season of unemployment, only to find closed doors at every turn. And then, I can't count the number of single girls I know who are waiting for God to provide husbands, or women of all ages who are waiting for healing from an illness.

Life can be brutally hard sometimes.

I don't want to spoil the book, but I not only survived my wilderness, I came out on the other side with one incredible story to tell. It's a great adventure . . . a wild frontier with some spectacular views. Along the way I learned some pretty amazing lessons. Lessons that I'd like to call "Wilderness Skills." Skills, because I'm pretty sure this isn't my last trek into the wild, and should I return, I've learned some things this go-around that I'll be certain to put into practice the next time I find myself lost in the outback.

Whether you find yourself facing loneliness or rejection, temptation or despair, I know this one thing for sure: the wilderness season you are facing will either make you or break you.

Hold on, my friend. Don't give up. You are not alone. Jesus also walked through the wilderness, and He has given us His Word as our map and Himself as our guide. I wish so desperately that I could hold your hand and teach you these skills myself. Try as I may, my words fail to give you my heart. I know your pain. I understand the brokenness. I've lived this thing . . . and the truths found in these chapters aren't mere theories . . . they are life.

chapter 2

The Wilderness
of Rejection

*Love is handing your heart to someone and taking the risk
that they will hand it back because they don't want it.*
—ROB BELL, *SEX GOD*

Call me weird, but I am a huge fan of Mondays. I look forward all weekend long to the start of a new week. No, I'm not one of those superambitious-can't-wait-to-get-to-the-office type of gals. There is only one reason for my eagerness: Monday means Girls' Night at my house. Giddy up!

Girls' Night

Just in case you ever join us, the rules for Girls' Night are as follows:

- No boys allowed. (AND . . . absolutely no cheating on Girls' Night to be with your boyfriend!)

- Arrive early if you want food. (Even though there is enough to feed a small village—without guys around we don't exactly eat like birds.)
- Make sure you are seated by 8:00 p.m. Prime seating goes quickly.
- All witty and clever commentary and predictions must be saved for commercials.

Preparations for our weekly gathering typically begin early Monday morning with e-mails flying back and forth from computers to "crackberries" and cell phones buzzing with text messages, all confirming one thing—*are we still on for tonight?* So . . . what exactly is it that draws us together each week with such glee and giddiness? No, I'm not talking about Monday night football or Bunko. The tradition that I share with you, which was labeled by one of my girlfriends as the "Cringe Fest," is the one and only, *The Bachelor* television show.

Yep, that's right, and I'm sure most of you know what I'm talking about. I'm out of the closet on this one. *The Bachelor* is my guilty pleasure (extremely guilty, I might add). There is nothing redeeming about it; it is junk food for the brain. I know this. I acknowledge that by watching this program I am shrinking my brain cells at a rapid pace. It is not good television, but at the same time, it is such *good* television! Granted, there are moments when I must change the channel due to too much hot tub exposure, but the same lure keeps drawing me and my girlfriends back for more. It is the lure of the "oh-no-she-didn't" moments. Or as one of our favorite blogs says in referring to the pathetic antics of the contestants, "Bless her heart."

Honestly, I really don't like the show. The guys are typically too cheddar cheesy for my taste. And as for the girls, well all

I can say is, "Darling . . . did you not see the television camera?" If eye rolling burns calories, then I am certainly getting a good workout in the hour-long program. So if I'm quite honest with you, my love for watching *The Bachelor* is not the show itself but the fact that once a week fifteen of my best girlfriends gather in my living room for two hours of nonstop, laugh-until-you-cry commentary.

"Did she really just say that?"

"Can he even hold a conversation?"

"Step away from the tequila, sister; this is on national television."

"Rewind that please; I *have* to hear that again."

"Doesn't she realize you can't trust what a man says to you in a hot tub?"

Good times!

But last night, after our usual Monday night festivities subsided, as I finished the last load of dishes and put away the remaining reminders that minutes before the house was filled with female laughter, a thought crossed my mind: *It's all fun and games till you are the girl left standing alone without the rose.*

Was this the voice of conviction? Was it the voice of guilt? Nope. I think the voice I heard while standing over my sink was the voice of empathy. Instead of shaking my head in disbelief at the craziness, I stepped into the stilettos of a girl who was just told she wasn't good enough to get a rose, and I felt her pain.

You see, each week's episode of *The Bachelor* ends with a gaggle of girls shedding tearful good-byes. Some are tears of gratitude that, yes, they would move on to the next round and not face the humiliation of elimination. But for the other girls, the tears are tears of pain. The real pain of rejection.

The coffee shop psychologist in me is always amazed at the reactions of the women on the show. It is fascinating to watch. Most of these girls have spent less than four hours total with the guy, but it never seems to matter. If she doesn't get the rose, she is totally crushed. And it doesn't really matter who the guy is . . . every girl wants to be picked. Not one single woman stands in the rose ceremony wishing that her name won't be called.

As women, we want to be singled out, chosen, and, yes, offered the rose. From kickball to homecoming queen, it never feels good not to be picked. But each episode of *The Bachelor* ends with one girl standing alone, empty-handed, and realizing her dream that she'd met "Mr. Right" ended when the last girl's name was called.

When you stop to think about it, all of the so-called reality TV shows thrive on this same formula. I know this to be true because in my house with four single girls we watch plenty of reality TV. One of my roommates is addicted to *America's Next Top Model* and another to *Dancing with the Stars*. All of us love to watch *American Idol*. There are others we don't watch, but the formula is the same: *Big Brother, Shear Genius, Top Chef*, and, of course, we can't forget the granddaddy of them all . . . *Survivor*. The basis of every single one of these shows is REJECTION! Whether it is Tyra Banks's dramatic monologue that ends a girl's hopes of stardom on the fashion runway or the crushing words "the tribe has spoken" that inform a food-starved contestant she has been officially kicked off the island—the end result is the same. One person walks away feeling like she doesn't have what it takes to be accepted. The contestant, model, dancer, house tenant, bachelorette, or singer is left knowing he or she didn't make the cut.

When was the last time you felt the bitter sting of rejection? If a camera crew secretly filmed your life, what scene would be your "rose ceremony"?

- A relationship ends, and you are left feeling hurt, alone, and quite unappealing.
- A divorce—your parents' or perhaps your own.
- Someone you love cheats on you.
- You feel like you just don't "fit" . . . too poor, too fat, too uncool, too _____.
- You are cut, eliminated, or fired.
- You are abused verbally, physically, or sexually.
- You are unjustly criticized or ridiculed.

Whatever it is for you, these moments in life can cause a torturous experience . . . the wilderness of rejection.

The Rose Ceremony

My "rose ceremony" of sorts occurred only a few short weeks after my boyfriend and I ended our long-term relationship. I, still anticipating the get-back-together stage of our relationship, was extremely naive to what was coming. I was at home when my best friend of ten years came over. She had that look on her face; I knew something was up. It was only two weeks from her wedding, and normally we would both be excitedly discussing her wedding plans. Yet, today she was somber and quiet. Sitting on the edge of her seat, she looked at me and said the dreaded words, "I need to tell you something." And in that moment I knew. Something in the pit of my stomach knew before the words left her lips. Then the knot that was in my stomach moved up like a boulder and crushed my heart as the statement, "He's dating someone," reached my ears.

I can't tell you the first words that came out of my mouth. They were not the nice, polite words of a good Christian girl who loves Jesus. I'm not proud of that moment. Looking back, I wish that I had stopped and simply praised God for His sovereignty and goodness, but I didn't do anything of the sort that day. I was an absolute mess—heartbroken, angry, and weeping. Truly, a pitiful sight.

As I stop and recall that day, I remember the pain—that searing pain of rejection. He—the guy I loved and thought I would marry—had picked someone else. I was living *The Bachelor*, and it wasn't at all funny.

To describe the months that followed as a "wilderness" is putting it mildly. In this time of intense pain and spiritual confusion, I turned to *the* guidebook for wilderness survival, the Bible, and discovered a life-changing truth.

Joseph

Seventeen. It can be such a fun age. I remember it well. You are no longer a child but not yet called to carry the full mantle of adulthood. It is a good year. That is, of course, unless you are Joseph. Then seventeen will be remembered as one pretty tough year.

Joseph is the son of Jacob, an extremely powerful and prominent man—a man of high calling and purpose. Imagine the pressure of your family line being Abraham, Isaac, and Jacob—the patriarchs of the Hebrew people.

> This is the story of Jacob. The story continues with Joseph, seventeen years old at the time, helping out his brothers in herding the flocks. These were his half brothers actually, the sons of his father's wives Bilhah and Zilpah. And Joseph brought his father bad reports on them.
>
> Israel [Jacob] loved Joseph more than any of his other sons because he was the child of his old age. And he made him an elaborately embroidered coat. When his brothers realized that their father loved him more than them, they grew to hate him—they wouldn't even speak to him. (Gen. 37:2–4 MSG)

We are introduced to Joseph by catching a brief glimpse at his dysfunctional family dynamics. Two words—sibling rivalry. Jealousy is the primary motivator here with Joseph and his crew of brothers—they loathe him because their dad favors him. For starters, Jacob gives Joseph this swanky multicolored coat. Now if you happened to attend Sunday school as a child, you will know this as the "coat of many colors." If not, just imagine your grandma's quilt with some armholes and a belt. (I know you want one too.)

To add fuel to the brothers' already roaring fire, Joseph has a unique gift. He is a dreamer and can interpret the dreams. One night young Joseph dreams his brothers will bow down and worship him. Now, I'm thinking he should have kept that bit of information to himself, considering the fact that he is not being voted most popular by his older brothers. He doesn't keep this dream a secret. Of course not, what younger brother would?

Joseph brags to his brothers of the dream, and this news causes them to hate him all the more. Jealousy is never pretty.

Then one day Jacob asks Joseph to go check on the older boys who are working a good distance away and bring back a report. Translation . . . Dad wants him to snoop on his brothers and let him know if they are behaving themselves. Can you think of a more perfect job for the already hated little brother? Now he gets to be the family narc. Sweet! Feeling mature and empowered with responsibility, Joseph obeys his father and heads out to find the guys. Little does anyone know that this assignment would bring about the worst day of Joseph's life. Or so it would seem from Joseph's perspective.

They [the brothers] spotted him off in the distance. By the time he got to them they had cooked up a plot to kill him. The brothers were saying, "Here comes that dreamer. Let's kill him and throw him into one of these old cisterns; we can say that a vicious animal ate him up. We'll see what his dreams amount to."

Reuben heard the brothers talking and intervened to save him, "We're not going to kill him. No murder. Go ahead and throw him in this cistern out here in *the wild*, but don't hurt him." Reuben planned to go back later and get him out and take him back to his father.

When Joseph reached his brothers, they ripped off the fancy coat he was wearing, grabbed him, and threw him into a cistern. The cistern was dry; there wasn't any water in it. (Gen. 37:18–24 MSG, emphasis mine)

Joseph was dumped in a pit in the middle of a wilderness. This is truly a wilderness of rejection if there has ever been one. His own family—flesh and blood—have rejected, forsaken, and abandoned him. That is putting it mildly. They despised him so much they wanted him dead. Ouch!

The Pit

I wonder what Joseph was thinking as he was hoisted over their shoulders and thrown into the bottom of that pit. Did he hope it was a prank that would end soon? Did he scream for release? Or, did he sulk and suffer his shame and humiliation in silence? Did he cry, or did his pride step in and deny his brothers the pleasure of his tears? Did he threaten to tell their father? Did he pray? Did Joseph ask God, "Why is this happening to me?"

Whatever Joseph did when his brothers threw him into the pit will remain a mystery, but the Bible tells us exactly what his brothers did while he faced rejection—they ate their supper. I'll be honest with you; this tiny bit of information irritates me. The injustice of it all! People don't tend to casually eat a meal when they are worried or concerned about someone. Rejecting their brother seems to be no big deal for these guys. The abandonment and the plot to murder Joseph is heartless, cold, and calculated, and they simply move on with business as usual. I can just hear them now, "Pass the lamb shank, please." "Why, certainly. May I have the salt?"

Will someone please tell me, *Who has an appetite while plotting murder?*

If I sound a little bit sensitive to their coldness, I suppose this part of Joseph's story brings to mind an all-too-familiar feeling from my own wilderness of rejection. There, in my own personal pit, my heart screamed out, *How dare you move on so casually while I'm bleeding over here? Can you not see what this is doing to me?*

But, oh girls, there is purpose in the pain!

Coincidence or Providence?

In the life of Joseph we see how purpose works even in the midst of his darkest moment. Joseph would have remained in that pit of rejection had not a golden opportunity crossed his brothers' path. A caravan bound for Egypt happens upon this dysfunctional family reunion, and its "chance" arrival spells life for Joseph. You may call it a coincidence, or you may call it providence, but one thing is for sure: Joseph's rescue from that pit came from an unlikely source and just in the nick of time.

> Then they sat down to eat their supper. Looking up, they saw a caravan of Ishmaelites on their way from Gilead, their camels loaded with spices, ointments, and perfumes to sell in Egypt. Judah said, "Brothers, what are we going to get out of killing our brother and concealing the evidence? Let's sell him to the Ishmaelites, but let's not kill him—he is, after all, our brother, our own flesh and blood." His brothers agreed.
>
> By that time the Midianite traders were passing by. His brothers pulled Joseph out of the cistern and sold him for twenty pieces of silver to the Ishmaelites who took Joseph with them down to Egypt. (Gen. 37:25–28 MSG)

I was never superb at math in school. I always preferred my language and history classes, but I can do simple arithmetic.

Divide ten brothers by twenty pieces of silver, and you discover that Joseph was rejected by each of his brothers for a measly two pieces of silver. Would that have even bought a cup of mutton stew in those days?

I wonder, did he ask the Midianite traders how much they sold him for? I wonder, did this knowledge taunt his heart as he realized how little he was valued by his own family? Was Joseph tempted to become bitter, jaded, and angry by the fact that his total selling price was less than the market value for a common slave? I'm sure he was tempted, but the amazing thing is the man we read of in the pages of Scripture exemplifies none of these characteristics. I wonder if on the back of that Bedouin's camel, in the midst of the sights and sounds of slavery, Joseph heard a still, small voice speak to his heart that said, *Trust Me. I am working all this for good. Your life is priceless to Me.*

I just wonder.

Danger Zone

There are untold dangers for a woman lost in the wilderness, but for the one who finds herself in the wilderness of rejection, a specific danger lurks—allowing the person, the parent, or the party who has rejected her to define her value and worth. For instance, someone close to me was abandoned at an early age by her biological mother. Although her adopted mom was wonderful, as an adult she walked through one tough wilderness as an identity of rejection surfaced in her relationships. She defined herself as unwanted and struggled for years to remove that false label. Another friend of mine sent me this e-mail after her recent breakup:

29

Dear Marian,

B—— and I broke up last night. Or rather, he started doing the Houdini (translation . . . when a guy suddenly disappears from the relationship without proper notice), and I finally called him on his fickleness. He said, and I quote, "I'm just not sure I'm ready to be in this relationship." Which we all know what that means, right? He is just not into me!!!! After all this time and this is what I get?

I feel sick. I'm miserable.

But the worst part is now I'm living with this monstrous self-hatred, and I feel so undesirable.

What's wrong with me?

Yours truly, A

Did you notice what my friend did? Her breakup caused her to question herself. Most of us have been there and know all too well the shock waves that a rejection strike can leave. She's far from being "undesirable"; actually she is beautiful, smart, and one of the godliest women I know. But rejection has a powerful way of fogging up our mirror of self-perception. A deep wound of rejection often leaves an insecurity that can result in devastating choices:

- For the young girl whose father walks out or was simply absent, the girl grows into a woman who feels unsure of her worth and looks from man to man to give her the validation she never received from her father. Sexual promiscuity often occurs from this type of rejection.

- When a woman feels rejected because of her appearance, she can feel worthless and turn to drastic measures to change. Eating disorders, fad diets, financial debt to keep up with trends, extreme plastic surgery, or body mutilation could result from feelings of rejection.

- For the woman in love who is rejected for another, she can feel inadequate and unlovable—in turn, settling for relationships that are abusive and destructive.

These scenarios describe the danger a woman faces when she allows another person to define her value. A breakup, abandonment, divorce, or dismissal can leave a girl feeling super insecure. But remember this: there is only One who is able and who has the right to define your worth, and that is God Himself. Women must beware of this danger when in a wilderness of rejection. The person who seems to have rejected you is not the one who defines you as a person. That right belongs to One and only One—your Creator.

I know this one from experience.

Weeks into my wilderness of rejection, my mentor called to tell me that she had a "word" for me. While praying she sensed the Lord leading her to tell me a very simple message. Three words, "You *are* lovable." She knew, as did my heavenly Father, that the breakup and consequent rejection were causing me to define myself by the actions or feelings of another.

The message the Lord wanted her to give me was, "You are not rejected . . . you are *accepted*." God alone defines my worth. I so badly needed to hear and believe those words. My thought life was under attack by the Enemy, and I needed a voice of truth to speak to me in the darkness.

In my wilderness I faced a huge choice: which voice would I listen to? The voice that delighted in telling me I was dispensable, unlovable, and rejected? Or would I listen to the voice of Truth, my heavenly Father, and walk in His definition of my worth? (Specific instructions on how to discern the voice of Truth and to silence the lies can be found in part 2 of this book.)

I tell you with full confidence and as one who has walked through this wilderness: God's opinion is the only important one, and He says you are loved, cherished, and yes, chosen. The love and acceptance found in Jesus Christ overrules every other opinion, evaluation, and criticism. Reflecting on the story of Joseph, I believe he must have understood this truth. For the man we see in Scripture is one who is confident. He knows who he is. His personal worth doesn't seem to be based on his brothers' opinions. Joseph is looking to a higher authority.

The "With You" God

The Bible tells us that once the caravan arrives in Egypt Joseph's brothers sell him to a man named Potiphar who is one of the pharaoh's officials. Here in Potiphar's house Joseph's character shines brightly for all to see, and the plan of God in this wilderness experience begins to be revealed: "As it turned out, GOD was with Joseph and things went very well with him. He ended up living in the home of his Egyptian master. His master recognized that GOD was with him, saw that GOD was working for good in everything he did. He became very fond of Joseph and made him his personal aide" (Gen. 39:2–4 MSG).

God was *with* Joseph. Often in the wilderness of rejection we are tempted to believe the lie that God has rejected us too. He hasn't. If you are a child of God, His love is always for you and He says:

> I have chosen you and not rejected you.
> Do not fear, for I am with you;
> do not be afraid, for I am your God.
> I will strengthen you; I will help you;
> I will hold on to you with My righteous right hand.
>
> (Isa. 41:9b–10)

As I walked through my wilderness of rejection, many times Satan tempted me to believe that God had abandoned me too—moments in which the pain was so intense that I felt forsaken. Yet, even in the darkest of hours, I knew God was indeed *with* me. I felt His strength when I continually faced seeing "them" together, or hearing of "their" engagement, or realizing that "our" friends had become "their" friends. I felt God's comfort when it seemed no one else quite knew how to heal my hurt. In times like these I would cry out to Jesus from the depth of my sadness, and I knew that He was indeed *my* Emmanuel (which, in the original language of the Old Testament, means "God with us").

One night as I read my Bible, a phrase jumped off the page that said, "He is the living God" (Jer. 10:10 NASB). *Living . . . God . . .* First of all, *living* means to "be alive." (Duh? No, I didn't need to go to seminary to figure that one out.) And then we have the word *God*. This is a word we use so flippantly that perhaps it has lost some of its weight and meaning. God . . . He is the Almighty, Sovereign, Creator, Ruler, Self-existent Being, the Sustainer of Life. That's powerful stuff.

As I read the words "Living God," my heart burst with joy, realizing that my God is indeed *living*. He isn't an enshrined deity far removed from my hurt and pain. No, Jesus is a God who has experienced life on this earth with its rejection and betrayal, and, yes, *He is alive* and *with me* in my time of need.

One of the greatest "with me" moments actually occurred a few weeks before my rose ceremony. I sensed a breakup was pending. My heart didn't want to let go, but I sensed it was only a matter of time. We were both seeking to hear from the Lord and to know what His will was for us. One night I tried to fall asleep, yet all I could do was pray, and I sensed God speaking these words to my heart:

> *You will be heartbroken.*
> *You will face rejection.*
> *You will be forsaken.*
> *You will feel humiliated.*
> *You will be abandoned.*
> *But remember,*
> *I am with you.*
> *For I, too, was brokenhearted.*
> *I, too, was rejected.*
> *I, too, was forsaken.*
> *I, too, faced humiliation.*
> *And I, too, was abandoned.*
> *I can walk this road with you because I walked this*
>   *road before you.*
> *I know the way.*
> *I am the Way.*
> *Follow Me.*

As God spoke these words to my heart, images of Jesus Christ flashed through my mind. I envisioned His best friends abandoning Him in the hours before the cross. I saw His own family reject Him. I saw the very people He came to rescue, abuse and ridicule Him, and I realized my God did understand the wilderness of rejection.

Trust me, girls, this was *not* the message I wanted to hear.

But later, when I experienced these things, I was comforted by the knowledge that Jesus, my Guide through this perilous land, had journeyed this wilderness before me. Right now, wherever you are—whatever you are dealing with—God is with you and, yes, He does understand. Don't despair. Cry out to Him. Allow Him to carry you through this wilderness. He promises to never leave you nor forsake you.

God was *with* Joseph and, yes, He is with you.

Not Karma . . . Destiny

Meanwhile, Joseph grows in favor in the house of Potiphar. God blesses him and everything he does. Potiphar, the master of the house, takes note of Joseph and places him in charge of his home. It seems Joseph must have been quite a cutie because Mrs. Potiphar takes a keen interest in him as well. Scripture tells us that time and again she attempts to seduce him, but Joseph makes it crystal clear that he is not that kind of boy. This woman is relentless, and she will not take no for an answer. One day she persists to the point that Joseph is forced to run from her presence.

Have you heard the expression, "Beware of a woman scorned"? It may have originated from this story. Potiphar's wife is now ticked off because she didn't get her way, and she is out for revenge. Like any good soap opera drama, this villainess fabricates a tale saying she was victimized at the hands of Joseph. The poor guy is framed! Once again Joseph finds himself in a horrible situation—falsely accused of rape and heading for the big house.

> When his master heard his wife's story, telling him, "These are the things your slave did to me," he was furious. Joseph's master took him and threw him into the jail where the king's prisoners were locked up. But there in jail GOD was still with Joseph: He reached out in kindness to him; he put him on good terms with the head jailer. The head jailer put Joseph in charge of all the prisoners—he ended up managing the whole operation. The head jailer gave Joseph free rein, never even checked on him, because GOD was with him; whatever he did GOD made sure it worked out for the best. (Gen. 39:19–23 MSG)

Whether in the pit or in the prison, God is *with* Joseph. In what seems to be the worst possible situation, God is at work. God positions him with the right people at the right time in order to fulfill a great purpose that even Joseph does not yet understand.

So we see that while in prison Joseph once again receives favor and his status is exalted from that of a common prisoner to the prison supervisor. This is where things start to heat up, yet from Joseph's perspective I'm sure they looked as bleak as ever.

Two guys are thrown into jail with Joseph. Both of these men work directly for the pharaoh. One man is Pharaoh's cupbearer, and the other his baker. In the course of their incarceration, they discover Joseph possesses the ability to interpret dreams. (Remember the "gift" that got him in this mess in the first place? It's about to come in quite handy.) Both men relate their dreams to Joseph, and he gives them an accurate interpretation.

Joseph explains his situation and asks the cupbearer to remember him when he is restored to his office. Sadly, Scripture tells us that he "did not remember Joseph" (Gen. 40:23). But God did.

Two years later. Two painfully slow years later, Pharaoh has a dream. Now the most powerful man in the world is in need of an interpreter. Pharaoh informs his household staff and finally, the cupbearer remembers . . . "That kid in prison . . . what was his name? Oh yeah, that's right . . . Joe something. Wasn't he that Hebrew slave? Whatever his name is, he interpreted my dream perfectly. Send for him immediately!"

Could this be Joseph's big break? Is this good fortune, good luck, or, as some would say, good karma? Nope, this isn't a matter of chance; this is what you call *purpose*. What we see here is an up-close look at God Himself moving, and His plan for Joseph is unfolding! After years of waiting, in a matter of minutes, Joseph transfers from the prison to the palace. He shaves, showers, and shines his shoes just in time to stand before Pharaoh himself. Ushered into his presence, Joseph hears the dream that is causing so much alarm. There are two dreams, but only one interpretation: "It is just as I said to Pharaoh: God has shown Pharaoh what he is about to do. Seven years of great abundance are coming throughout the land of Egypt, but seven years of famine will follow them. Then all the abundance in Egypt will be forgotten, and the famine will ravage the land. The abundance in the land will not be remembered, because the famine that follows it will be so severe" (Gen. 41:28–31 NIV).

Through Joseph, God warns Pharaoh that a great famine is coming upon the world. And Joseph also gives wise counsel concerning Egypt's response to this news:

"And now let Pharaoh look for a discerning and wise man and put him in charge of the land of Egypt. Let Pharaoh appoint commissioners over the land to take a fifth of the harvest of Egypt during the seven years of abundance. They should collect all the food of these good years that are coming and store up the grain under the authority of Pharaoh, to be kept in the cities for food. This food should be held in reserve for the country, to be used during the seven years of famine that will come upon Egypt, so that the country may not be ruined by the famine." The plan seemed good to Pharaoh and to all his officials. (Gen. 41:33–37 NIV)

Girls, this isn't a case of being in the right place at the right time. This is destiny! God brought Joseph to Egypt precisely for this reason. His gift is used to prepare a nation for a famine that is coming and to save millions from devastation. I wonder, does this truth dawn on Joseph as he gives the interpretation to Pharaoh?

The incredible thing is God doesn't stop with simply using Joseph to provide the information. No, God had an even greater purpose in mind and positioned him to be the second most powerful man in the world—the prime minister of Egypt. As Pharaoh said, "No one in Egypt will make a single move without your stamp of approval" (Gen. 41:44 MSG).

God, in His amazing sovereignty, prepared Joseph for this position. Joseph is part of a grand story that has been unfolding since the beginning of time—the story of redemption. It is now his time to take center stage and play the role he was born to fill. As the prime minister, Joseph is in a position to administer a food supply during a famine that will hit Egypt and all of the surrounding nations.

The seven years of plenty come and go, and during those years Joseph wisely manages the nation, storing food for the coming years of drought. The Bible says the food was "beyond measure" (Gen. 41:49). Then famine hits and it hits hard, but Egypt is ready. Yet, things aren't so cozy back in Canaan where Joseph's family lives. Joseph's brothers, who blissfully indulged in dinner as he cried in the pit, are feeling the pit of hunger; now they are the ones who have to cry out for help. And where do you think they turn? Egypt, of course.

Irony?

Nope.

God.

Jacob hears food is available in Egypt and sends his ten oldest sons there to acquire grain for the family. Little do they know that the very ruler they will bow before, begging for help, is the brother who had envisioned this very moment in a dream many years before.

Perspective and Sovereignty

Following the same path as the caravan that took Joseph into slavery, his brothers now traverse this well-worn route in hopes of finding lifesaving food. Upon their arrival in Egypt, they must face the prime minister and present their request to him, but these guys have no clue that the powerful man standing before them is the very brother they had rejected.

Scripture tells us Joseph instantly knew his brothers even though they didn't recognize him (Gen. 42:8). Disguising his identity, he peppers them with questions about their family and homeland. After several rounds of interrogations and sending them back and forth to Canaan, Joseph is finally undone with emotion, revealing to them his true identity and revealing to us an amazing perspective on the wilderness of rejection.

> Joseph spoke to his brothers: "I am Joseph. Is my father really still alive?" But his brothers couldn't say a word. They were speechless—they couldn't believe what they were hearing and seeing.
>
> "Come closer to me," Joseph said to his brothers. They came closer. "I am Joseph your brother whom you sold into Egypt. But don't feel badly, don't blame yourselves for selling me. God was behind it. God sent me here ahead of you to save lives. There has been a famine in the land now for two years; the famine will continue for five more years—neither plowing nor harvesting. God sent me on ahead to pave the way and make sure there was a remnant in the land, to save your lives in an amazing act of deliverance. So you see, it wasn't you who sent me here but God. He set me in place as a father to Pharaoh, put me in charge of his personal affairs, and made me ruler of all Egypt." (Gen. 45:3–8 MSG)

Strand by strand a tapestry is woven together to reveal a beautiful work of art. Likewise, our lives are woven by the most brilliant of all designers, the Lord God Almighty, who makes known the wisdom of His loving sovereignty as He takes the events of our lives and shapes them for good. When Joseph stands weeping before his brothers, he unveils for them the awesome plan of a loving God who allowed the painful rejection to occur so that a great and marvelous plan could happen

. . . one that would ultimately save them all. In the final chapter of Genesis, he says to them, "Don't be afraid. Am I in the place of God? You planned evil against me; God planned it for good to bring about the present result—the survival of many people" (Gen. 50:19–20).

OK, help me out here.

Is Joseph bitter? Nope.

Is he lashing out in anger? Not so much.

Is he seeking revenge for the pain he endured? Actually, he does the opposite.

Surprisingly, Joseph does not respond to his brothers with retaliation. Most people in his position would have relished the opportunity to make the ones who hurt them pay for their actions. But Joseph doesn't. Instead, he extends grace and offers forgiveness. How could he do this? He sees his experience through the perspective of God's sovereign plan and releases the ones who hurt him by saying, "What you meant for evil God has used for good."

What is Joseph saying here? I think if he were to sit down with you and me for a cup of coffee and chat about our heartbreaks, career upsets, and the ups and downs of life, Joseph would look at us and simply say, "Girls, what seems like rejection is God's protection." Do you see it yet? His brothers intended harm, evil, and rejection, but God used it for good.

Ken Gire states it so beautifully in *The North Face of God:*

> Joseph is an example of another way in which God
> reveals the mystery of his ways. Joseph spent most of
> his life not knowing why God had allowed his broth-
> ers to sell him into slavery, why he had allowed him to

be brought to a foreign land, why he had allowed him to be falsely accused and thrown into prison. From behind bars, it must have seemed so unjust. But from the summit of understanding that God later granted him, it all made perfect sense (Gen. 50:20). It was there he learned the seemingly meandering ways of God weren't simply leading to the shaping of his character but also to the saving of his family (a lineage that led to Christ), preserving them through seven years of famine and prospering them for generations to come.[1]

Ladies, repeat after me: what seems like rejection *is* God's protection.

Woman vs. the Wild

I have a little confession to make. I had somewhat of a crush on the star of the show *Man vs. the Wild* on the Discovery Channel. Just in case you've missed it, *Man vs. the Wild* is a documentary/reality TV show that pits one man—"Bear"—against the wild of nature. Bear (aka my wilderness crush) parachutes into harsh environments (Sahara desert, Alaskan wilderness, Hawaiian volcano), and he teaches the skills necessary to make it out alive.

In each episode Bear gives survival tips for those who find themselves in harsh terrain: tips such as how to find water, how to eat insects so that you can get plenty of protein, and how to build a snow hut. I did have to break up with my TV crush during one episode when he drank water from elephant dung. (Sick!) Nonetheless, I watch. All in all, Bear provides some very useful survival tips for those of us who consider our local jogging trail a wilderness adventure.

Man vs. the Wild proved to be quality research in my study of wilderness survival. I've thought about hosting my own show, *Woman vs. the Wild,* but it would mainly consist of me and my girlfriends in unfriendly terrains like shopping for shoes at a sample sale. And the only fresh salmon hunting we do is when we are trying to decide where to eat sushi. (I digress.) Not only did watching *Man vs. the Wild* prevent me from actually having to be stranded for days alone in a jungle somewhere, but it also allowed me to get top-notch wilderness training from the comfort of my very own couch. I love technology!

It never fails; in nearly every episode Bear begins with the same skill—when lost in the wild, find the highest point of elevation near you and climb to the top of it. Why? Simple, so you can gain perspective on your location.

Perspective is extremely important in wilderness survival. Perspective proves crucial whether lost in the Sierra Nevada or in a wilderness of rejection. Girls, as followers of Jesus Christ and daughters of the Most High God, whenever we face a circumstance that seems like rejection, we need to take a hike up a little mountain (actually it is quite massive, a summit that I like to call The Sovereignty of God) and look at our situation from that vantage point.

To say that God is sovereign means He rules and reigns over His creation—to know He is actively working and involved in your life and causing the circumstances of your life to work for a purpose. Translation: God isn't sitting up in heaven saying, "Oops, I really dropped the ball on that one."

This aspect of God's character is the rock upon which we stand in the wilderness of rejection. We do not fear, we do not dread, we do not lose hope because we know He *is in control.*

So, when the sting of rejection hits, we can say, "This circumstance was filtered through the sovereign hands of my God." We have this promise from God's Word: "God causes *all things* to work together for good to those who love God, to those who are called according to His purpose" (Rom. 8:28).

Hmm . . . Let's think about this one for a second. What would be included in that "all things" category?

A breakup . . . check.

Being fired . . . check.

Ridicule . . . check.

Not being picked for kickball . . . check.

Abuse . . . check.

Neglect . . . check.

Abandonment . . . check.

When God says "all things," He means *all things*. Recap. Think about how God worked all things for good in the life of Joseph. Consider these awesome facts, and see the greater purpose play out:

- If Joseph's brothers never sell him to the Midianites, then Joseph never goes to Egypt.
- If Joseph never goes to Egypt, he is never sold to Potiphar.
- If he is never sold to Potiphar, Potiphar's wife never falsely accuses him of rape.
- If Potiphar's wife never falsely accuses him of rape, then he is never put in prison.
- If he is never put in prison, he never meets the baker and butler of Pharaoh.
- If he never meets the baker and butler of Pharaoh, he never interprets their dreams.

- If he never interprets their dreams, he never gets to interpret Pharaoh's dreams.
- If he never gets to interpret Pharaoh's dreams, he never is made prime minister.
- If he is never made prime minister, he never wisely administrates for the severe famine coming upon the region.
- If he never wisely administrates for the severe famine coming upon the region, then his family back in Canaan perishes from the famine.
- If his family back in Canaan perishes from the famine, the Messiah can't come forth from a dead family.
- If the Messiah can't come forth, then Jesus never came.
- If Jesus never came, you are dead in your sins and without hope in this world.

What seemed like rejection truly was God's protection. When we choose to look at our circumstances from the summit of God's sovereignty, we are given the gift of peace that comes only from perspective. Granted, we may never know why some things happen. Knowing why is a rare gift that God sometimes gives to us—it is not something we are entitled to. Faith trusts Him when we don't get our reason.

Wonton Wisdom

Two cups of wonton soup, one order of sesame chicken, and a few spicy spring rolls. No, this is not my takeout order for a pitiful, home-alone Saturday night. This is the order for a lunch that brought my wilderness into perspective. I recall the table, the worn plastic menu, and the smell of Chinese food because it was at that lunch that God taught me a little thing about perspective on the wilderness of rejection.

I sat at lunch with a mentor of mine, giving her the play-by-play of my recent breakup and journey in the wilderness of rejection. Sipping green tea as she listened to my tale, she paused to ask, "Do you remember the story of Joseph?" I smiled, trying to be polite, yet thinking, *Yes, of course, I remember the story of Joseph.* (Slightly annoyed because I really wanted to talk about myself.) Until she said this, "Did you ever think about the fact that the caravan was on its way to Egypt long before Joseph was ever thrown into that pit?" I sat there for a minute, pushing my food around my plate as this life-changing truth settled into my soul.

God was at work and His sovereign plan was unfolding before Joseph's brothers even began to plot his murder. God, in His wisdom and sovereignty, ordained that the caravan bound for Egypt would cross their path just in time to rescue Joseph from facing death. Perfect timing. Not too late and not too early. God had a purpose for Joseph's life, so what seemed like rejection was God's protection. If that is the case, then the same applies to me. God was working and unfolding His plan for my life long before my heart was ever crushed.

A few months later I would understand why and celebrate God's goodness and His wisdom in allowing my heart to be broken. At lunch that day I still didn't know the reason, but I believed. I believed God was sovereign, and, yes, I believed He was good. And I understood that He had an amazing purpose in this wilderness of rejection.

I can't explain to you how amazing my sesame chicken tasted that day.

I'd been in the pit for months; food was the last thing I wanted. Then, all of a sudden, my appetite returned. I had a glimpse, just a brief glimpse, of the beautiful purpose of God in allowing the pain of rejection into my life. As I spooned another bite onto my plate, I thought, *I'm going to be just fine because my God has sent a caravan my way, and He is still on His throne.*

Recently, I taught "wilderness skills" to a group of girls in my city. We laughed, we cried, we shared our stories of broken hearts and bad decisions. At the end of the series, a friend brought something for "show-and-tell." Framed like a graduation diploma was a rejection letter from a world-famous company. Working for this business had been her dream job when she graduated from college. When she received the rejection letter ten years ago and read the words, "You are not selected for a position with our company," she was devastated. Today, my friend keeps this letter on display in her bathroom ('cause, girls, you know that's where we do most of our crying) so that when she is facing a rejection she can remember to see it as God's protection. You see, this company went on to be involved in a huge corporate scandal and eventually dissolved. Not only that, God had an entirely different path for my friend—one that she is uniquely gifted for and loves. Today she has perspective and is so thankful for the rejection because that meant a better plan—God's plan for her life.

Now, let's say it all together: "WHAT SEEMS LIKE REJECTION IS GOD'S PROTECTION!"

When we stop for a minute and look at rejection from the perspective of God's sovereignty, we realize:

- If I am not with that guy, it is because that relationship is not God's best.

- If I am rejected by that particular group of girls, then God had a really good reason for allowing that to happen.
- If I am rejected by that company, then God has a better plan or His purpose is different.

For the girl who is walking in God's will (obeying, trusting, and loving Jesus), she can know that the circumstances of her life are filtered through the sovereign hands of a God who knows her future, who knows her designed purpose, and who knows what He is doing. Even if she doesn't "get it" yet.

When rejection hit my heart like a bomb, I couldn't fathom the incredible purpose God had in allowing it to happen. My vision—being small, limited, and shortsighted—only saw my heart bleeding. But God saw my destiny. He saw His purpose for my life unfolding and how a broken heart would propel me to begin a ministry to reach women for Jesus Christ. He knew that His plan was better than my plan. I could never have seen that from my vantage point of pain. But looking back from a summit of understanding on the mountaintop of God's sovereignty—I CAN SEE!

And wow, is this view breathtaking!

chapter 3

The Wilderness of Temptation

*To be commanded to love God at all, let alone in the wilderness,
is like being commanded to be well when we are sick,
to sing for joy when we are dying of thirst, to run when our legs
are broken. But this is the first and great commandment
nonetheless. Even in the wilderness—especially in the wilderness—
you shall love him.*
—FREDERICK BUECHNER

There are many types of wilderness seasons that women can face. There can be painful seasons of grief or the tormenting pit of rejection or perhaps the hopelessness of despair, and most women will at one time or another know the excruciating wilderness of waiting. I don't know what you are enduring today, but one thing I do know for sure is this: in whatever trial you will face, there is yet another wilderness that attaches itself to every other one—temptation. The brand of temptation I refer to is not like the classic cartoon depiction of an angel on one shoulder and a devil on the other enticing the conflicted to choose between good and evil. No, that is too obvious. The one I speak of is much more subtle . . . but, oh, so dangerous.

I suppose I should confess to you my former naivete on this matter. I used to think of temptation as something that was clearly black and white.

To steal or not to steal?

To lie or tell the truth?

To eat yet another piece of key lime pie or to say no to the cellulite and walk away?

Those were the notions that fluttered around my brain when I heard the word *temptation.* But now, after following Jesus for some time, I've discovered that temptation is far more covert and seductive than I first believed. And when in a wilderness season, the deception one faces is not always easy to recognize. Trust me when I tell you that a girl can find herself lost in the backwoods of temptation and never know she left the city.

Let me tell you a little of my own story of facing temptation in the wilderness.

Head Over Heels

I flat-out fell head over heels in love. Yep, I was a goner. You actually may know him. Well—capital "H"—Him . . . Jesus. It may sound cheesy or even churchy, but this is my favorite way of explaining the radical transformation that occurred in my life nearly a decade ago.

To say I wasn't expecting this turn of events is an understatement. Sure, I'd grown up going to church, but mostly because my parents made me. Girls, let me just say I didn't know Jesus from Jose Cuervo. Actually, I knew Mr. Cuervo pretty well back then. I was what you would call a wild child—in every sense of the word. If there was a rule, I'd break it. If there was a way to get in trouble, I'd find it. If there was a booze with a guy's name (Jack Daniels, Johnny Walker, Jim Beam), I'd introduce myself, and if there was a blue or frozen drink . . . well let's just say I had a lot of blue tongues and head freezes back then!

All that changed, however, the day I met Jesus.

Before, I was the girl looking for love in bars, boardrooms, and bedrooms. And then . . . *wham!* Love found me. *The* Love that I'd been desperately searching for in all the wrong places found me. Before, I was grasping at anything and everything that I thought would make me feel whole, complete, or valued. The problem was nothing would ever fill the gaping hole inside of me that was crying out for God.

You could say I was a mess. Combine the consequences of my sin and the brokenness of my childhood, and you had one empty, bruised, and battered young woman. But you'd never know it by looking at me. From the outside, I looked like your typical young, single girl trying to find her next "fix"—a new guy, a new outfit, or just a new happening party scene.

Then I met Jesus.

I was absolutely blown away by the love and grace of God offered to me in Jesus Christ. Girls, I didn't find religion. No! Far from it. I met a Person. And He loved me. No, really, He L-O-V-E-D *me*. Mess and all. The irresponsible, absentminded, can't-find-her-keys, procrastinating, lying, insecure, drunk and promiscuous, messed-up childhood, party girl . . . *me*. *He* loved *me*.

But there was a huge problem in our relationship. . . . *I* didn't love *Him*.

51

Events from childhood and my own sin left me with a deep distrust of God. How could a "good" God have allowed the painful events of my past to occur? And because of my own rebellion and sin, my view of God was distorted. Here's the thing, sin darkens our understanding of who God really is; therefore, our image of God is marred. As a result, we don't trust Him. Or perhaps it was the fact that I was carrying a heap of shame, and I didn't believe God could forgive a girl like me.

I was in the midst of a major worldview shift. Part of me distrusted God, but the other part of me was beginning to see God in a new light. I had heard of His grace and forgiveness. Now I was beginning to see Him as loving and kind, instead of mean and punishing. Jesus was wooing my heart to Himself. I was a girl in conflict.

Could I trust this Jesus?

Should I surrender my life to Him?

Would my life really be rewarding if I followed Him?

I felt torn. My old life was broken, yet familiar. Following Jesus was an unknown—a step of faith into a mysterious world of surrender and obedience. I wanted to take the step . . . really I did, but there was something holding me back.

During this time I met a girl. She was beautiful, hip, and fun—not at all what I expected from a "church girl." We met at the church I was attending. Amy is her name, and the way she lives her life rocked my world. Amy invited me to join a Bible study group that met in her apartment. I went for a few weeks, and each night I left feeling miserable. Amy had something I did not have . . . she had a passionate love for Jesus Christ. Let me repeat myself. She was crazy in love with Jesus. So much so that she did silly things, like, I don't know, *obey*

Him. Amy based her lifestyle choices on her love for the Lord. Obeying God was simple because she loved Him. Trust me when I tell you that this line of reasoning was a totally foreign concept to me.

You see, at that point I believed obedience was something I *had* to do. I didn't realize that obedience was motivated 100 percent by love. If you love God, then you obey Him. So, there I was, a complete moral mess with no clue of what a relationship with God really meant—and yet still being pursued by Jesus. And sitting before me each week was this total Jesus freak.

But Amy wasn't weird; she was normal (which really jacked with my head all the more). That Bible study sincerely messed me up. I couldn't shake the feeling that something major was missing in my life. I wanted what Amy had.

She was passionate for Jesus.

She was filled with joy.

She wasn't empty.

She didn't live in the emptiness of hookups and hang-overs.

She truly desired to live a life that brought God glory.

One night I left her apartment after Bible study and sat in my car crying (imagine the really ugly face). I knew I couldn't go on the way I was living. The call of Jesus was so strong, yet the lure of the old and familiar was just as powerful. Even though I recognized my old life was empty, I still didn't trust that life with Jesus could actually be fulfilling.

Sitting in my car, I started talking to God. Not knowing how prayers were "supposed" to sound, I just said to God whatever I felt. Here is the conversation God and I had that night—the night my whole life changed:

Jesus. . . . [heaving sobs]

I don't know much, but I do know that You are real.

I can't explain all of this stuff that is happening to me, but I'm beginning to figure out that I can't get away from You.

I know You died for me, and I know You love me. But I also know this: I don't love You the way Amy loves You.

Frankly, I'm not sure I even like You all that much.

But I know myself. I am a complete failure at being "good." I know You are the only option for me. It's You or nothing else. I'm not going to find whatever it is I'm looking for anywhere but in You.

But here's the deal. If I am going to live my life for You, then You need to do one thing for me: GIVE ME A HEART TO LOVE YOU MORE THAN ANYTHING ELSE IN THIS WORLD! Trust me, this is the only way this relationship will work.

I know me. I'll go back to my old ways tomorrow.

There is no way I can live this life for You if I don't love You. Jesus, change me.

DO WHATEVER IT TAKES . . . but GIVE ME A HEART THAT LOVES YOU.

I had no idea the power of that prayer. My world turned upside down. Something supernatural occurred inside me that night. Today I know I experienced what God spoke of in the Old Testament when He said: "I will give you a new heart and put a new spirit in you; I will remove from you your heart of stone and give you a heart of flesh. And I will put my Spirit in you and move you to follow my decrees and be careful to keep my laws" (Ezek. 36:26–27 NIV). And also in the New Testament when He said, "If anyone is in Christ, he is a new creation; the old has gone, the new has come!" (2 Cor. 5:17 NIV).

Later, when I stumbled across these verses in the Bible, I thought, *THIS HAPPENED TO ME! I am a completely new person!* Today I realize I wasn't a phenomenon. God is in the "new creation" business. His specialty is taking girls like me and making us new—women with new hearts, new desires, and a new love—Jesus Christ.

I am a redeemed girl! God did give me the new heart and new desires, and I wanted with everything in me to live for Him. Something happened in my heart that night—I fell *crazy* in love with Jesus. Girls, I'm talking about butterflies. I was my worst nightmare. I was a Jesus freak and I didn't care.

Why do I tell you all of this? I belabor the point to say God answered my specific prayer. He gave me a heart that loves Him more than anything else in this world!

More than any guy

More than any possession

More than anything

Like I said, I absolutely fell crazy, head over heels in love with Jesus.

I simply must tell you the most amazing thing: the more I came to know Jesus, the more my love for Him deepened. My life didn't transform overnight. Every believer walks through a transformation process called *sanctification* (becoming more like Jesus in our thoughts, motives, and actions). This is an internal transformation of the heart, mind, will, and emotions when we choose to surrender to God's leading and follow Him.

Let's just say I needed a complete overhaul.

God, in His grace and mercy, wouldn't leave me as the insecure, broken, needy, wounded girl that He had redeemed. No, God loved me far too much to leave me in that condition. So for the next few years, I went through reconstruction as God:

Healed me from a childhood trauma

Renewed my mind from ingrained thought patterns of shame, self-hatred, and sin

Restored my soul

Cleansed me from past sin

Taught me to live as a new creation

Like I said, it was a complete overhaul.

Today I call myself a *redeemed girl* because that is exactly what I am—redeemed. I would never sugarcoat this one for you. Transformation wasn't and still isn't easy. I had to make a choice to pursue wholeness. Sure, the renovation of my soul was wrought with pain as I faced the issues of my past, but this season was also filled with tremendous joy because, in it, God was making me whole.

Here's my point. At every stage of healing and transformation, my love and passion for Jesus increased exponentially.

How much does the captive love the One who sets her free?

How much does the debtor love the One who pays her debt?

How much does the sick love the One who heals her?

How much does the one who is lost love the One who finds her?

As Jesus said, "The forgiven much love much" (Luke 7:47 paraphrase). And oh, girls, did I experience the "much." Over the years Jesus became my Healer, Friend, Shepherd, Rock, Redeemer, Rescuer, Restorer; and as I jokingly replied to every person when asked if I was dating someone, "Jesus is my boyfriend."

Oh yes, by the way, throughout the years of transformation, I was also extremely single. I was so busy serving God, the years flew by. Sure, I had my share of dates and occasional crushes, but I never opened my heart to anyone.

That was, of course, until, you know . . .

"Betrayed"

That relationship was my first serious one as a Christian woman. It was the first time I'd allowed my heart to take the plunge. And when I tell you I sought God as to whether I should take this proverbial leap—*seeking* is an understatement. Girls, I'm not lyin' when I say I prayed my guts out. I read Scripture. I sought wise counsel.

I'll be honest, I was a little scared. I was such a total mess in the relationship department before I met Jesus that I did not trust myself one bit to make a smart choice on my own. I was the girl who could pick the biggest loser a mile away. So, I sought God. Seriously. I did not at all want to be outside of God's will one bit in this department.

During my years of transformation, or what should be called the *real* Extreme Makeover, I would tell God over and over again that I only wanted His best. I didn't want to waste my heart or my time on any pointless relationships. I was a redeemed girl, and I desperately wanted to do things "right" this time around.

So, as I sought the Lord I sensed He gave me the green light. I trusted that I was 100 percent in God's will in entering that relationship. One day as I was studying the Bible, I felt God speak clearly to me from the Word concerning this guy, and knowing this gave me the assurance to allow myself to fall in love.

Today, given time and the gift of perspective, I realize there were so many reasons *why* the Lord purposed that season of my life. He did speak to me. I was 100 percent in His will. But back then, during the painful heartbreak and while still wandering in the wilderness of rejection, I had plenty of questions. Girls, I did *not* understand why. For the life of me, I couldn't figure out why God led me to do something that He knew full well would only result in my heart breaking.

To say the least, I was confused. The outcome did not make sense to me. And then I realized that if I was following God's will, that meant, *Oh no . . . God allowed this pain to enter my life. No, it wasn't that God simply allowed the pain; it seems He must have purposed this wilderness.* That truth was a hard one to swallow.

Friends, it was a dark, dark time.

My words flat-out fail to describe for you the turmoil in my heart. Just thinking back to that season causes a pit in my stomach. Writing about that darkness evokes memories of my misery. This broken heart certainly wasn't my first trial as a Christian. I'd walked through many a wilderness before, but this was the first time I felt betrayed by God. Yes, I said that word—*betrayed*—and it was sheer agony.

I knew God was sovereign, which meant He allowed and

purposed the circumstances. I also believed with all of my heart that He had the power to change the situation. Knowing this about God caused me to expect that He would act on my behalf the way I thought He should. I believed He could and would intervene. My belief system told me God is able to change hearts, bring reconciliation, and fix problems. So when God did not meet my expectations and when I understood He had purposed my pain, the resulting feelings of betrayal almost destroyed me.

Can you relate to my turmoil? Have you ever felt like your trust was betrayed? If so, keep reading.

Realizing my heartbreak was an "act of God" hurt the worst. The One I loved the most chose to inflict a deep wound to my trusting heart. Please hear me: I knew I wasn't "supposed" to feel this way. Hence my agony. My turmoil had nothing, absolutely nothing, to do with the guy. This was between me and my Redeemer—the One I loved with all of my heart. And in this wilderness, my heart longed to praise Him, to bring Him glory through my reactions, and simply to remain faithful. But my mind . . . oh my mind, it was filled with questions:

- Why did You allow this to happen to me?
- I thought You loved me.
- If You love me so much, then why I am in this place?
- Where did I go wrong?
- Do I really know how to hear Your voice?
- Should I choose to trust You and to follow where You lead me if this is the destination?

A battle raged around me. I was in a war. And this, girls, was a war for my worship.

The War

Weeks into the wilderness I knew something dark and sinister was stirring. Doubts and questions about God's goodness, faithfulness, and love that I normally never struggled with seemed to hiss and snarl at me from every turn. Please don't think I'm paranoid or anything, but I really felt like I was being followed. Something evil crept in the dark corners. Just when I was doing great (i.e., making it through a whole day without a meltdown), the questions began sneaking into my thought life. Although in the moment I didn't fully comprehend my situation, now looking back I know the Enemy, Satan, was prowling.

Then one day I heard a sermon by Louie Giglio about worship. To paraphrase, Louie said, "We (humanity) are worshippers. That is why we were created, and that is what we do. It's not a matter of *if* you worship. You do worship . . . the question rather is who or what do you worship?" So I'm listening, nodding in agreement, when Louie said the words that just about knocked me off my chair. "And right now, wherever you are, there is a war going on over your worship."[2]

Suddenly my circumstances made perfect sense. I was living in the middle of a battlefield! Even though camouflage was on its way out of style, I was seriously considering purchasing a whole new wardrobe. I was in the battle of my life, and, frankly, at that point I was losing miserably. My passionate love for Jesus Christ was under attack. And the question the Enemy of my soul kept asking during those dark days was this: "So, how much do you love Jesus *now?*"

Louie's message exploded like a truth grenade. I was in a war. Satan—the Enemy of God, the Deceiver, the Accuser of the Brethren, and the Father of Lies—wanted me to bail on loving Jesus. It would delight Satan if I would cease worshipping God when life didn't turn out as I planned. I know this is his motivation because robbing God of worship has always been Satan's number one desire.

Before I dive into how Satan seeks to destroy worship through a wilderness of temptation, I first must address one crucial question: *What is worship?* To quote Louie yet again, "Worship is our response to what we value most."[3] I like that definition. For in it we find two important words. The first is *response.* Worship is a response to God for who he is and what he has done. The other word is *value.* Value is simply ascribing worth to something. That is what worship is—we are saying to God, "You are worthy of my life, my praise, my all."

Now that we know that we all are worshippers, it would be a good thing to understand what exactly each of us is worshipping. Perhaps the best way to figure out what we worship is to figure out *what it is we value most.* Is it a person or perhaps a possession? Is it a career, a calling, or maybe a reputation? Wherever you or I invest our time, money, and emotions . . . that, my friend, is what we worship. When I think of whom or what the object of my worship is, I ask myself, "What is at the center of my life?"

Now that we know what worship is, let's take a look at how Satan seeks to destroy our pure worship of God through temptation. From the very beginning Satan has used the same exact strategy to entice worshippers away from God— temptation. In the garden, Satan did this by causing doubt about God's goodness, questioning God's truthfulness, and tempting Eve to distrust God. The temptation? Turn away from God and put something else at the center of her life—herself.

Eve, believing Satan's lie that God is not good, chose to turn away from Him and to remove Him from the center of her life. This was Satan's strategy in the very first temptation, and frankly, his mode of operation is still the same today.

Here's my point. Behind every temptation of the Enemy lies a question: *Can God be trusted?* For example, when you are tempted to break a commandment of God (e.g., sex outside of marriage, lying, or envy), somewhere in the back of your mind are a few questions: *Does God really have my best interest at heart? Can I trust Him? Don't I know what's best for me?*

And when a believer is facing a wilderness season (heartbreak, disappointment, rejection, loneliness, despair, or unmet desire), the Enemy sees an easy target for his faith assault. In our moments of weakness, he bombards believers with accusations about God's goodness and trustworthiness. His primary goal is the destruction of the close relationship that his target has with Jesus Christ. Satan knows full well he cannot do one single thing about our salvation, but that does not stop him from trying to rob God of our worship. Have you ever been, or are you currently, that target?

The Test

Stories abound of individuals who walked with God until the big storm hit. In their time of suffering, a distrust of God arose in their hearts, and they turned away from Him. In my years of ministry, I've seen countless women forsake their relationship with Jesus during a heartbreak or when waiting for

Mr. Right took longer than they planned. God, it seemed, was not doing as He was "supposed" to do, and, therefore, they chose to walk away from following Him.

I now understand why. A Predator in the wilderness seeks out the hurting and the wounded, hoping to inflict a deathblow to the one thing that will actually sustain his prey in their time of need—their faith.

Before my recent wilderness, I could never understand how a woman could walk away from Jesus. I suppose I should repent of my judgment. Not until I faced the Tempter head-on did I understand the intensity of his assault. Not until I experienced the war for my worship did I realize how sinister and manipulative the Father of Lies can be. Now I know in seasons of suffering that there is something huge at stake—*Will you still worship and love the Lord in the midst of the wilderness?* No one in human history knows this fact better than a man named Job.

Girls, I want you to stop right now and consider the worst possible tragedy you could face. What is it? Is it the death of a loved one? Or perhaps financial ruin or false accusation? Would it be a crippling disease? Now, imagine the pain, the agony, and the desperation you would feel in that situation. What if every possible scenario happened at once? Now, that's what I call a wilderness. This intense level of suffering was the plight of Job, the most famous wilderness wanderer of all time.

The Bible says Job feared God and served him wholeheartedly. (*Fear*, in this context, means "to honor, revere, and worship.") Job was a prehistoric Jesus freak. Little did he know it, but one day his passionate love and worship of God were the topic of discussion between the Lord and Satan. Their chat went a little something like this:

Satan: "I think Job only worships You because You are good to him. Take away his blessings, and I know he'll curse You to Your face."

God: "Let's see about that. You can strike him, but you cannot kill him."

Satan desires to discredit God as worthy of worship, so he suggests that Job is a perfect example of his theory. As Philip Yancey says, "Satan scoffs that God, unworthy of love in himself, only attracts people like Job because they're 'bribed' to follow him. If times ever get tough, Satan charges, such people will quickly abandon God."[4] While the worthiness of God is the issue up for debate, the real person on trial is Job.

Job's trial begins with one horrific day:

- In a flash, all of his wealth is destroyed: 7,000 sheep; 3,000 camels; 500 oxen; 500 donkeys.
- Wiped away are his servants, his homes, and all of his possessions.
- Tragically, all of his beloved children are killed: seven sons and three daughters.
- Then, just to make matters worse, Job breaks out in painful, whelplike sores from head to toe. Job's health—gone.
- Finally, his wife goads him to "Curse God and die!" (Job 2:9 NASB).

And you thought you were having a bad day!

Now for the test: *who* will Job worship? A gauntlet thrown down and attached to it a question: "Will Job love God or curse Him? Will he trust God or deny Him?" In the midst of Job's suffering and pain, the Enemy ambushes him with the temptation to curse God.

The word *temptation* can be interpreted two ways in the Bible. One means incitement to sin, and the other means to test or to prove. Both definitions of temptation apply in Job's situation. Satan is tempting him to sin, while God is allowing him to be proven faithful.

James Dobson, in his best-selling book *When God Doesn't Make Sense,* describes the seasons of testing perfectly:

> Most believers are permitted to go through emotional and spiritual valleys that are designed to test their faith in the crucible of fire. Why? Because faith ranks at the top of God's system of priorities. Without it, He said, it is impossible to please Him (Heb. 11:6). And what is faith? It is the substance of things *"hoped for, the evidence of things not seen"* (Heb. 11:1 KJV). The determination to believe when the proof is not provided and when the questions are not answered is central to our relationship with the Lord.[5]

I love how Dobson describes faith: "the determination to believe when the proof is not provided." That's it! That is the issue in the wilderness. Satan tempts us to distrust God's character, and God watches to see if we will believe. Will we worship when all reason and evidence are gone? Will we continue to love Him and trust Him in the trial?

So, in Job's life the question raised was *"How will he respond?"* I realized in my wilderness that the temptation to doubt God and bail on Him was a test—and perhaps somewhere the question was raised, "How will Marian respond?"

So, how did Job respond to this suffering? The Bible tells us, after learning of the death of his children and destruction of his wealth, Job worships.

Then Job arose and tore his robe and shaved his head, and he fell to the ground and worshiped. He said,

"Naked I came from my mother's womb,
And naked shall I return there.
The LORD gave and the LORD has taken away.
Blessed be the name of the LORD."

Through all this Job did not sin nor did he blame God.

(Job 1:20–22 NASB, emphasis mine)

Worship

In the Bible, worship is not primarily about singing songs or acts of devotion. It is about one thing: offering a sacrifice. Something is placed on the altar and dies. When Job, in the midst of his suffering, falls to the ground and worships, he offers God a sacrifice. What is his sacrifice? After carefully and prayerfully reading his story, I believe the sacrifice made by Job that fateful day was this: the expectation to have life on his terms.

Job expresses his worship in an offering of words when he says, "Though he slay me, yet I will praise him" (Job 13:15 paraphrase). Complete surrender. Unwavering devotion. And this offering proves a crucial victory in the war that raged over his worship.

God=1

Satan=0

Even though Job never wavered in his worship, that doesn't mean he didn't ask questions. As Philip Yancey says, "When people experience pain, questions spill out—the very questions that tormented Job. Why me? What's going on? Does God care? Is there a God?"[6] Yancey points out, "Throughout the book of Job he does question *why*. Sure he asked questions, but his fidelity to his God remained."[7] Honestly, one of the things that astounds me about Job's story is that he has no clue a wager had gone down over his life, yet Job still didn't allow the Enemy to steal his affection and devotion.

Job's suffering was catastrophic. I would never compare the wilderness I walked through to a Job-like season. But I do know I experienced a similar temptation from the Enemy:

- To curse God
- To turn away from Jesus and find a new lover of my soul
- To bail on worshipping my Redeemer when life didn't go according to my plan

That, my friend, was the seductive temptation the Father of Lies set before me in my wilderness season.

Mascara Worship

For months, with mascara smearing down my face, I worshipped the Lord through tears. I don't say this to pat myself on the back. No, I tell you this because worship was a battleground. The worship I speak of is corporate worship—when the people of God gather to praise God.

I love to sit on the front row in church—partly because my ADD-self is less distracted if I sit close but also because I like to be near the action. But as I walked through the wilderness, my pride hated the front row because it became a public display of my misery. There's nothing like going into meltdown mode on the front row of a megachurch to boost one's self-image.

Everything in me wanted to hide the battle going on within me. To just pretend I didn't care. I wanted to be aloof, removed, unaffected, to appear to those who saw me as "doing great." But I wasn't. I was hurting, and despite my best efforts to seem fine, I was fragile. Like I've said, I've never been one prone to tears, but now, all of a sudden, I was a Kleenex commercial.

During my wilderness season, engaging in corporate worship was a choice. For weeks I would walk into the sanctuary of my home church with that "I'm doing great" smile plastered across my face, find my seat, and then the music would begin. And each week, without fail I might add, we would sing:

> *Blessed be Your name*
> *When I'm found in the desert place*
> *Though I walk through the wilderness*
> *Blessed be Your name*

(lyrics by Matt Redman)[8]

The irony never failed to register. These are the very words of Job. I would stand in worship and crumble inside when the song began. I learned quickly that singing "Blessed be the Name of the Lord" is a choice of the will. To sing His praise and to give Him glory in the midst of heartache is a sacrifice of praise. I would sing these words with tears racing down my face.

Tears of frustration

Tears of embarrassment

Tears of brokenness

Tears of worship

The battle was intense, and the mascara sure burned my eyes, yet I was not about to let the Enemy steal my worship. I fought. I lifted my hands and sang the words until the storm raging in my soul was quieted by the conviction of my will. To believe. To simply believe—despite how I felt in the moment or what I could see with my eyes—that my God is good and, yes, He *is* worthy of my worship.

At some point in the wilderness of temptation, I realized this truth: *there was no better way for me to express my love to God than by staying faithful to Him in my pain.* Remember how I said I fell flat-out head over heels in love with Jesus? Well, I guess this would be one of those times when my love was put to the test.

I recall one night as I was weeping before the Lord and asking why, I could hear the Enemy taunting me and whispering for me to go back to my old life because at least there I would be "in control" and I could "protect myself from pain." In that moment my mind flashed to a story in Scripture. It was the moment when Jesus became unpopular with the people of Israel.

Prior to this time He had hundreds of followers. When Jesus was the "miracle man" and the "popular speaker," everyone wanted a piece of Him. But when the heat turned up and His teachings became tough, the masses turned away. Then Jesus looked at His few followers that remained and asked, "Will you go too?" There is that question again. *Will you bail on Jesus when times get tough?* Now the disciples faced the choice—to love or to leave, to worship or to walk. I absolutely love Peter's response: "Where would we go, for you alone have the words of life?" (see John 6:66–68).

Long before I fell in love with Jesus and even longer before I walked into my recent wilderness, a woman named Hannah Hurnard wrote a much-beloved tale called *Hinds' Feet on High Places.* In this book Hurnard tells the journey of Much-Afraid as she follows the Shepherd (Jesus) to the High Places and how she overcomes her tormenting fears and doubts. This story is an allegory of the Christian life and of the various wilderness experiences we encounter in our spiritual journey with Jesus.

In this tale Hurnard perfectly depicts the tormenting temptation to abandon following Jesus when enduring an intense heartbreak. Much-Afraid, well into her journey to the High Places, turns a corner and faces The Valley of Loss (the name itself describes the pain one endures when entering this valley). As Much-Afraid peers down into the valley, she panics and is tempted to stop following her beloved Shepherd. Much-Afraid draws a profound conclusion:

> For one black, awful moment Much-Afraid considered the possibility of following her Shepherd no longer, of turning back. She need not go on. There was absolutely no compulsion about it. She had been following this strange path with her two companions (Sorrow and Suffering) as guides simply because it was the Shepherd's choice for her. It was not the way which she naturally wanted to go. Now she could make her choice. Her sorrow and suffering could be ended at once, and she could plan her life in the way she liked best, without the Shepherd.
>
> During that awful moment or two it seemed to Much-Afraid that she was actually looking into an abyss of horror, into an existence in which there was no Shepherd to follow or to trust or to love—no Shepherd at all, nothing but her own horrible self. Ever after, it seemed that she had looked straight down into Hell.[9]

Like Much-Afraid, I peered down the corridors of time and pictured my future with Jesus and without Him. For a brief moment I considered the life I left behind—a life of emptiness, shame, and regret. I didn't have amnesia; I knew life without Jesus was far worse than any trial I could ever face with Him. If I didn't have Jesus, I didn't have anything. That night on my bedroom floor a decision was made. Despite the pain, despite the confusion, despite the accusations of the Enemy, I was sticking with Jesus! Although at that time I still didn't "get" God's big plan, I knew I would never find joy or happiness apart from Him.

That night the Enemy lost the war for my worship.

God=2

Satan=0

A decision was reached; I would continue to love Jesus, for God did not have to tell me *why* in order for God to be good! Whether I am married or single, broken or whole, humiliated or adored, God is worthy of my worship, simply because of who He is.

chapter 4

Sarah . . .
A Survivor's Story

You have turned for me my mourning into dancing; . . .
That my soul may sing praise to You and not be silent
O LORD my God, I will give thanks to You forever.
—PSALM 30:11–12 NASB

My friend Sarah is every woman's nightmare. I say this as a huge compliment to her.

For starters, she is drop-dead gorgeous. Then to add insult to injury, she is super sweet—the "are you for real?" kind of sweet. If that isn't enough, the girl's got talent. Not, "so your mom thinks you're talented" kind of talent. No, Sarah has some serious skills. She can sing, and she can flat-out dance like nobody's business. Each week she uses her talents leading children's worship at our church. Did I already mention she is beautiful? It's simply not fair.

I tell you all of this because I learned a powerful lesson from a recent conversation with Sarah. Drumroll, please . . .

NEVER EVER, NEVER EVER, JUDGE A BOOK BY ITS COVER!
Gee, I know, I'm original.

Seriously, I thought I had Sarah pegged. She's pretty, petite,
and seems just about perfect. She has an amazing family, an
awesome job, an adoring husband—the whole enchilada.
Judging by externals, I imagined her life was carefree and easy.
I looked at Sarah and thought, *She doesn't know one thing about
the wilderness.* I was wrong. For the record, I was *so* wrong!

One night Sarah was hanging out at my house, and while
we were talking I asked her if she'd ever had a wilderness experience. (Asking questions and living with myself prove to be
my greatest methods of research.) We'd only associated casually before this night, and my image of her was constructed
from who she was on stage. I knew her as the bouncing blonde
who sang and danced hip-hop for Jesus. So when I inquired
about her testimony, I suppose I should confess that I already
had Sarah stereotyped. Since I've been honest so far, let me
paraphrase for you what I expected to hear:

So . . . like, I was born to the perfect family and
I grew up to be a cheerleader. The big wilderness
season of my life came when I didn't make head
cheerleader, but God carried me through that one.
So, like, I went to college and was involved in some
great ministries there before landing the perfect job.
That is where I met my perfect husband. Like, isn't
God good?

That was the testimony I anticipated. Like I said, I'm an
idiot. Don't judge a book by its cover. What she said actually left
me speechless, which if you know me is a rare thing, indeed.

I sat for over an hour and listened as Sarah opened her heart and told of a season in her life that can only be called a wilderness. As she spoke, every preconceived notion fell away, and my respect for her grew immeasurably as I heard what she had survived.

Sarah has survived the wilderness of temptation (along with rejection and despair), and this is her story:

I grew up in a Christian home with a wonderful family. Mine was a happy childhood. I was active in soccer, cheerleading, gymnastics, and show choir. Anything that I tried out for I made. I had tons of friends and was involved in an awesome church youth group. Everyone knew if you wanted fun, love, and Jesus, you could find it at our house. My family would travel together every summer serving in medical missions in El Salvador.

Life seemed to be . . . well . . . perfect. That is until my sophomore year in high school when I was taken into the darkest wilderness I have ever experienced. I hit rock bottom multiple times and constantly prayed for the Lord to just let me die.

I was sitting in class when suddenly I had this intense burning on my skin. It felt like someone was taking sandpaper and rubbing into an open sore. That day I was rushed to the doctor to hear one thing, "Nothing is wrong. Everything is normal."

I was far from normal.

As the year passed, I visited a plethora of doctors and my physical issues started increasing. I began having heart palpitations and sweating profusely, causing me to roll down the windows when it was snowing outside because I felt like I was on fire. Yes, fire. Often I would feel dizzy and faint, but that wasn't the worst part. Oh yes, by the way, I started drooling. Just what a sixteen-year-old is hoping will happen. Then, one of my eyes started drooping. (Oh so perfect for prom pictures!)

My heart was burning, and breathing became so difficult that my mom had to start sleeping in my room because I had such trouble getting a single breath that she would need to rush me to the ER. Then I began having headaches that were so powerful that I could not lift my head. And all the while the intense burning continued.

Then I lost control of my bladder. I was sixteen years old and wetting the bed! Embarrassing doesn't begin to cover this one. If I stayed at a friend's house, I had to sleep on a trash bag just in case I had an accident.

Doctor after doctor left me and my parents without answers. Some physicians said it was all in my head, and one guy even told me to just breathe into a paper bag. More than once my doctor visits ended with me in a ball on the bathroom floor bawling and feeling completely defeated.

Finally, the Mayo Clinic discovered I had postural orthostatic tachycardia syndrome (also known as POTS). This diagnosis explained the dizziness, fainting, sweating, breathing issues, and tiredness, but it did not explain the burning pain or the headaches.

Meanwhile, physicians from all over the United States continued to perform test after test, procedure after procedure, prescribing medicine after medicine, and ordering multiple surgeries. I always left without any answers or pain relief. After each visit I felt more defeated and more hopeless. Sometimes I would weep for hours and wouldn't be able to eat, talk, sleep, or function.

During that season the only thing I wanted was for my heavenly Father to take me home. I really did want to die. Honestly, I felt like life was just not worth living. Yet, every time I got to that point of despair, the Lord managed to pick me up out of my misery and get me walking again. I sensed Him saying, "Get up and walk, for I have not finished My work in you yet." The Lord spoke to me in my brokenness and gave me the strength to keep going.

Finally, a doctor discovered my nerves were firing more rapidly than they were supposed to, and this malfunction caused the burning pain. Although he did not know why or how to stop it, I at least felt freedom that it wasn't just in my head. After this discovery, a physician diagnosed me with Arnold-Chiari malformation (ACM), which is a rare genetic disorder in which parts of the brain are formed abnormally.

Some of the most common symptoms of ACM are intense headaches, burning or numbness of the skin, difficulty swallowing, blurred vision, blind spots, and bobbing of the eyes.

At last, we knew the cause for all of my symptoms. In my nontechnical terminology, this condition is when the opening is too small at the base of the skull between the brain and spinal cord. The opening doesn't allow spinal fluid to flow through the canal. The only way to correct the malfunction is through brain surgery.

Meanwhile, as I am going through all of these medical issues, my life is changing drastically. I could not play soccer anymore because of my headaches. I struggled very hard to continue singing in choir, but during performances I would either sweat profusely or pass out. My school work suffered because the pain would be so severe that I would need to leave school.

I longed to be a normal teenager.

This is when my friendships starting changing. My "friends" spread rumors about me. Some reported that I had some sort of awful disease, while others said I was making it all up for attention. Most just said I was crazy. My "best friends" tried to get me kicked off the cheerleading team because they thought my "disease" would drag them down. I can't tell you how much this rejection tore me up inside.

When I did have brain surgery, one of my "friends" told the class I wasn't really in the hospital. She said I lied because I wanted out of school for seven weeks. Needless to say, I went from popular to pariah.

This wilderness was lonely. I didn't understand why the Lord was allowing me to go through this. I thought to myself, *I'm a good girl. Why me? I don't drink, use drugs, or have sex like most of the other high school kids. I'm involved in my youth group and place my relationship with the Lord as my highest priority.*

I remember thinking, *How could God let this happen to me? What did I do wrong?*

Through this time I felt depressed, rejected, lonely, and hopeless. I thought, *I will never live a normal life. I won't go to college, get married, have a family, or function with any kind of normalcy.* I feared I would live with my parents or in a hospital for the rest of my life. I dreaded being poked and prodded by needles, cut open and sewn back up, medicated and dependent on people forever.

After my brain surgery (such a fun way to spend the junior year of high school), fourteen out of sixteen of my symptoms were gone. Glory to God! The burning pain and the headaches remained. I spent seven weeks out of school in recovery. Once the seven weeks of recovery ended, the headaches were gone, but I was still stuck with the chronic burning pain, which I still live with on a daily basis. Again, I began another roller-coaster journey as I sought healing from pain for which no cure has been found to this day.

During my wilderness experience I began questioning God. Not if He was real, but more so, I'd ask, "Why me?" When my illness progressed and I suffered physically, Satan tempted me to believe all sorts of lies about God and His character. I went through periods where I believed God was punishing me for something. I was tempted to believe that He had completely abandoned me, or the worst lie, that God actually enjoyed watching me suffer.

In these times I would cry out, "Where are You? Why don't You answer me? If You are the God of peace and comfort, why do I feel this way? If You are a God who heals, why are You choosing not to heal me?"

One night I was pounding my fist on the floor; I was so mad at God for "rejecting" me, for saying no, and for leaving me in the dark. I couldn't understand why He didn't answer me and was so content to watch me suffer when all the while He had the power to stop my pain. As I was crying out to Him, in a vision I saw Jesus weeping. My God was weeping with me and over me. It seemed Jesus was in more pain than I was and was truly broken over my suffering. His tears revealed His heart.

In that moment, I knew my pain had a purpose or God would not allow it. We live in a broken world that is filled with sin and suffering. God is not sadistic. Satan wanted me to believe He took pleasure in my pain. The truth is Jesus aches for me. I know God was saying to me, until healing comes, "My grace will be sufficient for you, and My strength will be made perfect in your weakness."

Today I no longer see my pain as torture but as an opportunity. In my suffering Satan tempted me to hate God and choose bitterness, but now I know that my joy is found when I love God and choose to worship. I've realized that through my illness I can bring glory to God. Every morning I wake up, and though it is physically excruciating to put my feet on the ground, I rise because God calls me to use my feet to dance.

It's a miracle; every day He gives me this supernatural strength. If it were for my own strength, I know I would be in a wheelchair by now. But the Lord, He gives me endurance, power, and perseverance, so that no matter how I feel, I can dance!

I suppose you could say my "wilderness skill for women" is choosing to worship. I have lived with suffering and allowing it to control my life. I have also lived with suffering while praising Him and allowing God to give me freedom and strength. Living the second way, I can pick up my feet, despite the severe pain, and dance before Him with the untouchable joy.

Girls, get this. Sarah should not be walking. She probably should not be alive today. Yet Sarah is the leader of a worship group called the Jump Team. God is a miracle worker! Every day He performs a miracle in Sarah by giving her the strength and the ability to do what He has called her to do—bring Him glory through her gifts and talents.

I love to watch that girl dance. Her feet move from a source that is otherly. Each step is a beautiful act of worship that brings glory to her King. During a dark season of life, Sarah made the choice to praise God with her life and with her talents, and by doing so she turned a wilderness of temptation into an act of worship.

chapter 5

The Wilderness of Despair

If you lose hope, somehow you lose the vitality that keeps life moving, you lose that courage to be, that quality that helps you go on in spite of it all. And so today I still have a dream.
—MARTIN LUTHER KING JR.

We also rejoice in our afflictions, because we know that affliction produces endurance, endurance produces proven character, and proven character produces hope. This hope does not disappoint, because God's love has been poured out in our hearts through the Holy Spirit who was given to us.
—ROMANS 5:3–5

The weather outside seemed to somehow perfectly match the topic of our conversation. It was raining a slow drizzle that caused everything to appear a dreary gray. The lack of sunshine cast dullness on everything. Huge raindrops splattered about us as my friend and I dined outside under the covered awning of a local breakfast dive. She was in a reflective mood but not because of the weather.

"I had to check *that* box yesterday," she began.

"What box?" I said, oblivious to the fact that checking boxes was something one did. I tend to ignore all forms of paperwork whenever humanly possible.

"THE OVER THIRTY-FIVE BOX!"

"Ohhhhh . . . ," I replied, with a mixture of sadness and dread, now fully realizing the implications of *that* box.

"And then I cried the rest of the day," she said softly, watching the rain fall on the pavement.

All I could do was look down at my oatmeal and say, "I'm so sorry."

That Box

Why did *that* box feel like the end of the world? What gives one little square so much power over a woman's emotional state? For my friend, it was more than just a little box; it was a category that seemed to scream, "Yet another year has gone by without your heart's desire being fulfilled. You are now thirty-five years old and nowhere near where you thought you would be at your age!" Although I don't know from personal experience, I can say with full assurance that *that* box is evil.

We all have "that box" that inflicts pain. What does yours say?

- overweight
- unemployed
- single
- infertile
- divorced
- failed

- disabled
- pregnant
- widow
- terminal

As we continued to watch the rain, my friend explained the despair she felt after marking herself in a new age bracket. "I felt myself giving up any sort of hope that my dreams would be fulfilled. Why bother? I guess I started looking back at my life, the choices I've made, the regrets, and the letdowns, and I asked myself, *How did I get here?*"

Obviously, being thirty-five and single was *not* her plan for her life. More than anything in the world my friend wants to be a wife and a mother. I don't know of a woman who believes in marriage more passionately than she does. She said, "I believe I was created to have babies, and each year that passes by, my chances of having a child get slimmer and slimmer."

"Despair," defined simply, is the state of being without hope. And without hope . . . a woman is then without joy. As my friend talked, she described the downward spiral of emotions she felt as her hope of marriage and a family seemed to become more of an ever-elusive dream.

Can you relate to the feelings of despair that my friend described? Have you ever been at the point where you were ready to give up hope completely? In the wilderness of despair you may often encounter loneliness, isolation, and pain, but always hopelessness. Perhaps you once hoped for a marriage that is altogether different than the one you find yourself in. Perhaps the career path you've chosen doesn't match the life you envisioned. Or maybe, like my friend, living with an unmet desire is sending you into the wilderness of despair.

I want to tell you my friend Catherine's story. She is a woman who endured unbelievable heartache and walked through the wilderness of despair. Her experience is an example of how heartbreak can strike in a moment and the importance of knowing what to do when those feelings of hopelessness hit:

Blood.

There was just so much blood. I am not talking about a little bit that you could wipe off with toilet paper. No. This was buckets of blood, pouring out of my body, splashing up onto my shirt, down onto my legs, and all over my hands.

I had always wondered why women got so upset over miscarriages. It was hard to imagine that someone could get so attached to something they had never seen before, much less held, talked to, etc. Well, now I knew. When the horrifying amount of blood began pouring out of me, I knew exactly what it was—my baby. There wasn't even time to process all the reasons I should be sad: the hopes dashed, the fertility suffered, the money gone. I just let out this visceral cry of pain. It made my sleeping husband jump out of bed.

Once at the hospital, the doctor confirmed it. There no longer was a baby inside me. They had tried to encourage me that maybe the bleeding was caused by something else, yet I knew. I just knew.

I just couldn't stop sobbing. The nurse offered me water, pain reliever, prayer. I said I would take the last one. God had not forgotten me. There, holding my hand, was my personal angel. I still couldn't stop sobbing, and they needed me to wait for the doctor, so they moved me to a room where I wouldn't scare the other patients.

I remember thinking as I sat in the VIP room (of course, I wasn't feeling very VIP), that I was on the edge of an abyss of despair with one toe already in. I prayed and asked God for one sentence that would be my rope back to Him, to sanity, to hope. It really wasn't the verse I wanted, but I couldn't afford to be too choosy at that point. He said, "The LORD is good and his love endures forever" [Ps. 100:5 NIV]. So that is what I said to myself over and over, probably at least a hundred times before the doctor came. Honestly, at first I didn't feel it. God didn't feel good, and I didn't feel loved. But after clinging to the verse for a while, it began to feel like the only truth—the only thing I could hold onto.

It was the truth—God's Word—that Catherine held onto like a lifeline in the moment of despair. In the Bible there's another woman who is desperate for a word of hope. Desperate for her own lifeline. Her story gives us insight into God's heart for those of us who find ourselves in a wilderness of despair. This is the story of Hagar.

The End of the Rope

Abandoned and miserable, Hagar sits down by a tree and waits to die. Hagar is the picture of a woman who is at the end of her rope. What trial has led this young woman to feel so discouraged?

Hagar is the maidservant of Sarai, the wife of Abram (later called Abraham). God promised Abram and Sarai (later, her name was changed to Sarah) that he would bless them with descendents and through Abram's family the whole world would be blessed. Theologians call this promise the Abrahamic Covenant. (A *covenant* is a fancy Bible term that simply means a promise or a contract between two parties.) The terms of this covenant were simple: God made a promise to Abram, and all he had to do was believe it. Well . . . time passed and Sarai did not conceive. They waited and waited as the years passed by, and the promise of God for a child seemed to be unfulfilled.

Let me interject right here with a word: *God's delays are not God's denials.* Perhaps your heart despairs because you, too, are looking at the proverbial biological clock and beginning to lose hope about your future. Let me give your anxious heart a word of hope . . . nothing, absolutely nothing, is impossible with God. He is not limited by time or biology. He is the God of the impossible. He loves, absolutely loves, when the deck is stacked against Him, for then He can do His God-stuff: miracles.

Mrs. Abram didn't seem to get this memo, so impatient Sarai decided to take matters into her own hands. Sarai "suggests" to Abram that he produce an heir through her maid-servant, Hagar, who would serve as a surrogate mother for the now elderly couple. This practice was considered normal according to the custom of that day, but this was NOT God's plan for Abram. Sarai thought, *If God isn't going to give me a child, then I'll get one for myself.* Abram agreed with Sarai, and the Bible tells us their impatience and her manipulation was detrimental to everyone involved:

> Abram agreed to what Sarai said. So after Abram
> had been living in Canaan ten years, Sarai his wife

took her Egyptian maidservant Hagar and gave her to her husband to be his wife. He slept with Hagar, and she conceived.

When she knew she was pregnant, she began to despise her mistress. Then Sarai said to Abram, "You are responsible for the wrong I am suffering. I put my servant in your arms, and now that she knows she is pregnant, she despises me. May the LORD judge between you and me."

"Your servant is in your hands," Abram said. "Do with her whatever you think best." Then Sarai mistreated Hagar; so she fled from her. (Gen. 16:2b–6 NIV)

Hagar finds herself in one tough jam. For starters, she didn't ask to be the surrogate mother. As a servant, she really didn't have much say in the matter. Sure, she was wrong in mocking and belittling Sarai when she did get pregnant, but does this constitute abuse? Sarai is undone with anger because of her jealousy. Hagar's mocking insulted Sarai, and she began to punish Hagar severely for her insubordination. In response to this harsh treatment, Hagar flees into the wilderness . . . literally, the wilderness of despair.

Lace on Hagar's hiking boots for just a minute and try to imagine the desperation she feels. Alone—in a day and age when women had nothing. No income. No source of food or shelter. No protection. I'm sure she felt completely abandoned. And for the cherry on top, she is pregnant. Yikes! How will she provide for herself, much less a child? Despair is understandable; her situation seems absolutely hopeless.

A Divine Search-and-Rescue Mission

Yet, there in the wilderness Hagar has an encounter. She is not alone. She is not abandoned. She is not without a Protector. Someone has come looking for her, and that Someone is God. I guess you could call this a divine search-and-rescue mission: "The Angel of the LORD found her by a spring of water in the wilderness, the spring on the way to Shur. He said, 'Hagar, slave of Sarai, where have you come from, and where are you going?' She replied, 'I'm running away from my mistress Sarai'" (Gen. 16:7–8).

Girls, when we are alone in the wilderness, God comes looking for us. I absolutely love this aspect of God's character. Just when we are at our breaking point, when we feel all alone and truly believe that no one understands or cares about us, God comes to our rescue. He does it for Hagar. She doesn't run into the wilderness searching for God, but He comes there intentionally looking for her.

The previous passage of Scripture tells us that the Angel of the Lord found Hagar by a spring of water. Throughout the Bible, the Angel of the Lord is believed to be a revelation of Jesus Christ before His incarnation (that's a big theological term for when God became a man—see John 1:1–14). This only occurs a few select times in the Old Testament, so translation, ladies . . . this is a really big deal! God loves the hurting and the oppressed, and He chooses to reveal this aspect of His nature to a woman in the wilderness of despair.

Two significant things happen in their encounter. First of all, when He speaks, He calls her by name: "Hagar." Can you imagine what this small act must have meant to her? In her culture, as a female slave, she was totally unimportant to the world, and yet God Himself calls to her and speaks her name. Girls, that means He *knows* her name and she matters to Him.

The Bible says the Angel of the Lord "found" her by a spring of water. We have a God who seeks to find the lost. He searches after the weak. He fights for the broken. God went looking for Hagar.

Are you running, hoping someone will catch you?

Do you, like Hagar, feel unimportant and overlooked?

Do you feel defeated by life?

Is "LOST" more than just a television show in your world?

Spill Your Guts, Girl

When the Angel of the Lord finds Hagar, He then asks her a question: "Where are you going and where are you coming from?" When I first read this story, I stumbled over that question. Puzzled, I thought, *Why does God ask her this? It's not as if God has stopped being the all-knowing One. God knows everything. Right?*

Then it clicked. God knows the answer to His own question, yet He inquires for Hagar's sake. When He says, "Hagar, where are you?" I believe God does this for relational purposes. You see, our God is relational, and what makes a relationship work? Communication! God asks Hagar this question so that she will open her mouth and tell Him about her situation.

I truly believe God desires the same from you and me when we are in a wilderness of despair. Our relational God (you know, the One who paid the ultimate price for our salvation with His Son's death, so that you and I can call Him "Father") desires for us to communicate the anguish of our hearts to

Him. Why are we hurting? What is causing the pain, the fear, and the suffering?

My friends joke all the time that "communication is my love language." It is so true. If they have scoop, then I want to be in the know. It makes me feel important, loved, and involved. I don't want to hear secondhand that a girlfriend is pregnant or promoted; I want to hear straight from the horse's mouth. Communication is my love language, and I think it is God's too. He communicates His love to us in so many ways, and I believe He loves it when we share our hearts with Him. That includes our questions, our fears, our pain, even our ickiness.

When the Angel of the Lord asks Hagar, "Where are you going?" He opens the door for communication. And guess what? Hagar walks through it. In very simple words she says, "I am running away from my mistress, Sarai." Sure, she doesn't say much, but in this communication she relates her circumstance to God, the injustice of the situation, and how dejected she is now feeling.

In the wilderness of despair, we don't need to hold back talking to the Lord about our pain. Women, by nature, are talkers. Duh? We *love* to share our struggles, but the problem is we so often spill our guts to everyone but God. During my recent trip into the wilderness, I found myself repeatedly turning to my friends and my family instead of the Lord.

Then one particularly bleak day I picked up my cell phone to call a friend, and I sensed the Lord saying, "Tell Me." Snapping the phone shut, I realized I was leaning on my friends instead of on Jesus. I turned off my cell phone for the afternoon and went for a jog. Sitting by a creek near my house, I talked to the Lord about the despair my heart was feeling:

I don't think I can take this anymore.
Do You realize how difficult this is?
Do You know how humiliating this is?
Will You please take this pain away?

Girls, here's the thing . . . through Jesus Christ we have the relationship with God for which we were created. We are designed by God and for relationship with Him. Our souls need our Maker. We *need* to relate to the Almighty, to communicate our hearts to Him.

In my wilderness season, I learned to let my guard down and to be weak, vulnerable, sad, and lonely with the One who already knew the state of my heart and loved me anyway . . . my Savior. During that season I learned to share my heart with God through prayer in a whole new way. These were not the pretty, polished, perfected prayers of high church. Oh no, these were the straight-shooting, no-holds-barred, tell-it-like-it-is kind of prayers. Messy . . . but real. And guess what? My rawness didn't shock God. Truth be known, the gut-level prayers took my relationship with Jesus to a place I hadn't experienced before.

One of the primary blessings of any wilderness season is the deepening of a woman's relationship with Jesus Christ. Honestly, I know Jesus far better today after walking through heartbreak with Him than I ever did before. He listened. He comforted. He counseled . . . like no one else could. As Psalm 34:17–18 states, "The righteous cry out, and the LORD hears, and delivers them from all their troubles. The LORD is near the brokenhearted; He saves those crushed in spirit."

During those months there were several nights I cried myself to sleep because I was so heartbroken. But over and over again, I would repeat to myself part of Psalm 73:28, "The near-ness of God is my good" (NASB). Half plea, half prayer, I'd say the sentence again, "the nearness of God is my good." I'd just say it until I could sense His nearness and feel His comfort. His peace would quiet my tears, and I would drift off to sleep. Now that I think about it, that's one of the great things about Jesus. You can call Him at 2:00 a.m. when you are in a full-blown meltdown, and not only does He actually take your call but He doesn't even complain about you the next day at the office. That's what I call a friend!

In research for this book, I've watched more documentaries on wilderness survival than I care to admit. The guys at my local movie store are beginning to think I'm a little "off" . . . if you know what I mean. I've read numerous tales of survivors in the wilds of Africa and horror stories of weekend expedi-tions gone bad. Real bad. All of these accounts have one thing in common: the breaking point—the place where despair sets in for the one stranded or lost in the wild. After hours or some-times days alone, the survivor has a moment of realization—*no one hears my cry for help.* It's one thing to be lost and alone . . . it's quite another thing to think no one is looking for you and no one hears you when you cry.

Do you ever feel invisible? Do you ever feel like no one knows what you are enduring? Do you feel like no one cares? The Lord not only searches for you in the wilderness, but He also cares deeply about your situation. Even if you've brought some of this trouble upon yourself through your own foolish decisions, He still cares! God knows your name. He understands where you've come from and where you are going. Jesus wants to bless you with the assurance that He is the God who sees.

The Lord Hears Your Cry

If I could only say one thing to women who find themselves in the wilderness of despair, it would be this—THE
LORD HEARS YOUR CRY! I know that the hardest thing about
a wilderness is feeling that no one understands, no one can
relate, and no one hears your cry for help. Let me say for the
record, God hears, sees, and, yes, understands your situation
more fully than you do.

Hagar experienced this truth in her wilderness, and the
next part of her story is a word of hope to any woman experiencing despair:

> Then the Angel of the LORD said to her, "You must
> go back to your mistress and submit to her mistreat-
> ment." The Angel of the LORD also said to her, "I will
> greatly multiply your offspring, and they will be too
> many to count."
>
> Then the Angel of the LORD said to her:
> You have conceived and will have a son.
> You will name him Ishmael,
>   for the LORD has heard your [cry of] affliction.
> (Gen. 16:9–11)

As believers we never need to feel that hopelessness. In a
relationship with God, we have the assurance and the comfort
as a child of God that He hears us and longs to rescue us.
When this truth dawned on Hagar, she celebrated this fact
by naming the place where God found her in memory of that
moment: "So she named the LORD who spoke to her: The God
Who Sees, for she said, 'Have I really seen here the One who
sees me?' That is why she named the spring, 'A Well of the

Living One Who Sees Me.' It is located between Kadesh and Bered" (Gen. 16:13–14).

What was it exactly that lifted Hagar out of despair? First, it was a clear revelation of the Person of God. And second, the realization that God, the Holy One, saw, heard, and understood her plight. Hagar found hope for her future because she had faith in the God who fully knew and understood her present. It was hope (optimism for the future) rooted in faith (believing God and His promises) that lifted Hagar out of her despair.

Hope and Faith

Hope and faith are the two lifelines that a woman needs when tarrying in that desolate wilderness. If hope is the very thing needed to lift a soul out of despair, then she better be able to trust who or what she places her hope in. The woman who desires a child cannot place her hope in fertility treatments. The sick cannot place their hope in physicians. The single girl who desires to be married can't place her hope in her appearance or any other physical thing. For a woman to have unfailing hope, she must place her hope in something other than herself. Hope, the kind that doesn't disappoint, must be rooted in an absolute for it to carry her soul out of the wilderness of despair.

Hope is the by-product of faith. If a woman doesn't have faith, then she certainly will not have hope; therefore, she will remain stuck in the wilderness of despair. But what is faith? The Bible says, "Faith is being sure of what we hope for and certain of what we do not see" (Heb. 11:1 NIV). Two powerful words pop out to me whenever I read this verse. First, is the word *sure,* which implies confidence and being fully persuaded that the desire will be met. It's having the guarantee of what you hope for. The other word that stands out in this definition of faith is *certain*. No doubt. No question. No confusion. Put these two powerful words together and you have a good picture of faith. A woman of faith has certain assurance.

Next question: why does faith matter? Faith matters to you and me because the Bible says, "Without faith it is impossible to please God" (Heb. 11:6a). Faith, confident assurance, pleases God. It says to Him, "I believe You are who You say You are, and I believe You can do what You say You can do." Ultimately, faith is rooted in God.

So, last question: how is it, then, that faith produces hope? Faith results in hope when a woman walks in confident assurance, her eyes are set and focused upon the unchanging and unwavering Person of God, and she believes that the outcome will ultimately be for her good.

People are fickle.

Medicines fail.

Relationships fizzle.

But God . . . He is faithful.

When a woman places her faith in God, she hopes in the One who is reliable. She believes in Someone who does not fail. She trusts in Someone who is rock solid. Every other place a woman puts her hope is unpredictable, but God is the sure thing!

Maintain Focus

Back to breakfast. My dejected and box-checking friend sitting before me this dreary, rain-drenched morning believes God. She has a strong relationship with Jesus and loves Him deeply. And I could tell from her demeanor that the despair from the day before was gone. I asked, "So, how did you pull yourself out of the funk?" After taking a long drink of coffee, she set her cup down and told me the rest of the story:

As I cried and cried, I finally heard myself. I was moaning and complaining, and the sound of it became sick to my own ears. "Why God? When God? Blah, blah, blah, blah." Self-absorption is so very depressing. So I decided to get up and go for a walk. While I was out, I began speaking truth to my heart. You know, I just started saying Scripture out loud. I started reminding myself of what I know to be true. I said to myself:

I believe God loves me.

I believe He knows and understands my situation.

I believe He is in control and has a purpose and plan for my life—even if I can't comprehend it fully right now.

I believe He knows the desires of my heart and He loves to bless His children.

Something happened as I spoke Scripture after Scripture and truth after truth to myself. The despair slowly lifted like a cloud, and my hope returned. You want to know the cool thing? As I turned to walk back home, I looked up and painted across the sky was this beautiful rainbow. Coincidence? I don't think so. Maybe I'm crazy, but I think God put it there just for me. When I saw it, I felt this tremendous peace flood my heart. A peace that said, "God does see me. God does hear my cries. My heavenly Father does care about me and He knows my desires and I know

I can trust Him." And from this peace came a spark of something else, a feeling that was familiar yet distant; it was the return of hope. And just as the rainbow follows the rain, joy followed hope.

Gloom lifting, I returned home. Still single? Yes. Still waiting? You betcha. But not in despair. Why? Because I will always have hope as long as I choose to believe who God is and what He has said to me in His Word.

The wilderness of despair happens when our emotions spiral out of control, which usually is the result of hopeless thinking. Therefore, if we choose to set our minds on God, to remind ourselves of His goodness, power, and glory, then our emotions will follow course. This isn't "the secret" or the power of positive thinking. Rather, it is taking action to reign in uncontrolled emotions with the Truth.

chapter 6

Cristy . . .
A Survivor's Story

*I would have despaired unless I had believed that I would see
the goodness of the LORD in the land of the living.*
—PSALM 27:13 NASB

"Could you tell me what happened that day?" I asked as Cristy and I sat at an outdoor café drinking coffee. Looking past me toward a young couple playing with their dog, she paused briefly, smiled as her eyes turned to meet mine, and said, "It began quite silly, really. I think we argued that morning about cookies."

It was a hot Thanksgiving Day in Texas. I know it was hot because we were both wearing shorts in late November. We'd only been married a little over a year, and we were still very much in the honeymoon season. Everyone called us Ken and Barbie. John really did look like Ken. Handsome, athletic, gregarious, kind, and full of life. Everyone loved him . . . especially me. Soon after we married, we began building our first house together. From slab to ceiling, we planned and purchased the whole project side by side. We were so in love. It's still painful to recall how happy we were.

Nothing could have prepared me for what would take place that day. It was a beautiful sunny day—without a cloud in the sky. We were just two young people in love, enjoying the many firsts of married life. As we drove to his parents' home for Thanksgiving lunch, I recall him eating my grandma's cookies—I teased him that he would ruin his appetite. Of course, John didn't care. John lived in the moment, and in that moment he wanted cookies.

He delivered bags of groceries to a needy family for their Thanksgiving, then we drove to his family's to celebrate the holiday with them. When we arrived at his parents' home, his brother was there, too, and with him a new toy . . . a motorcycle. John, always up for a new thrill and challenge, decided to take it for a spin. Immediately, I was concerned, and as he walked out the door I asked, "Do you even know how to ride that thing?"

A little nervous, I reasoned, *But he's a professional athlete. Calm down; he'll be fine.* So I went about getting lunch ready and put it out of my mind. Several minutes later his brother bounded back into the house in a panic, yelling, "Hurry, there's been an accident!" My first thought was, *John has broken something.* An arm . . . perhaps a leg. I bolted out the front door, and as soon as I crossed the threshold something came over me. A wave of sickness flooded me—as if my spirit knew what was coming. My chest dropped into my stomach . . . I can only describe it as a looming dread.

I sprinted as fast as I could to the street, and as soon as we reached the scene of the accident, I knew. Even though at the time everything in me denied it and willed the opposite, the minute I looked at him, I knew he was gone.

The man I loved, the man I thought I would spend the rest of my life with, raise kids with, spoil grand-kids with . . . had died.

I'm embarrassed to even call my season of heartbreak a wilderness when I hear my friend Cristy tell her story. This is real suffering. I know people say you can't compare pain, but if there is a contest, she wins. Hands down. I don't know many people who've tasted a tragedy of this proportion.

I knew I was treading on sacred ground, but after her reassurance that she wanted to share her story, I asked, "What happened next?"

I needed God to breathe.

The days that followed are a blur, really. I think I was in shock. Initially I was numb. I could barely function. I don't know how I physically stood to walk and attend the funeral other than the fact that the Lord carried me.

In the weeks that followed, getting out of bed was a difficult task. I would fall to the ground from the pain—it was so physical I would get violently ill. I didn't know if I would live through the grief.

I can honestly say I sensed God's presence in a

powerful way. I knew I wasn't alone. I literally didn't
know how I would get through minute by minute.
. . . I fell down in grief dry heaving. . . . All I could do
was cling to God. I had an amazing family, but no one,
absolutely no one, could carry me but Jesus.
"How was this season a wilderness?" I asked tentatively.

Despair. I was in utter despair for a while. I didn't
see a light at the end. I didn't have hope for the future.
That, to me, is a wilderness. But besides those emotions I also struggled with the questions. The questions just about drove me nuts. Mainly, I asked myself,
"What if?" What if we'd made other plans? What if I'd
been more firm? I also struggled with the "why" questions. Why did this happen to us? John and I served
in the church; we followed God's ways. In my mind
it wasn't supposed to happen this way. Those types
of questions seriously bombarded me until I came to
peace with God's sovereignty. I rested in the fact that
God had a purpose for this that I could not understand right now. I know it sounds cliché, but this
knowledge gave me an incredible amount of peace.

Aside from the questions, I also had to grieve. Just
allow myself to mourn the loss—this was a process.
Looking back, I could have easily gotten stuck in
depression for the rest of my life. It is one of the stages
of grief, but it is not supposed to be our destination.

Despair was ever present. At such a young age to
lose your husband and have that type of happiness
ripped away, I remember thinking I never wanted
to be happy again. I said these words to my dad one

afternoon, months after John's accident, as we were driving in the car. My dad looked at me and said, "Then you don't have the faith that you profess."

When Dad said those words to me, I knew he was right. I realized living in despair is living in hopelessness. Until that day I'd never stopped to consider that I could have hope and joy ever again.

After that conversation, I thought long and hard about what it was that I did believe. What was this thing that I called "my faith"? I believed there is a God. I believed He is good and sovereign and that His plan was good. I also believed that God gave His Son to die for me, so He understood my loss and pain. Just stopping to think about my faith, what I truly believed, gave me the hope to make it the next day, and then to the next.

My life verse from that season was Psalm 27:13: "I would have despaired had I not believed I would see the goodness of the Lord in the land of the living." Believing in the goodness of God in the midst of my suffering was the only thing that lifted me out of despair. It was my light in the darkness. Believing was the source of my hope and, consequently, my joy.

Now, several years later, Cristy can authentically testify to the power of faith. How believing God pulled her out of the darkest days of misery. Her story illustrates in many ways what the Bible teaches us about despair and how to overcome it. She is a girl who knows firsthand that God is faithful, and, yes, she has seen the goodness of God in the land of the living.

chapter 7

The Wilderness
of Unmet Desires

*Desire is the source of our most noble aspirations
and our deepest sorrows. The pleasure and pain go together;
indeed, they emanate from the same region in our hearts.*
—JOHN ELDREDGE, *THE JOURNEY OF DESIRE*

My flight to Los Angeles was scheduled to leave in less than two hours. If everything went according to plan, I would leave my house for the airport with plenty of time to fill up with gas, find a place to park, take the little parking shuttle to the terminal, breeze through security, stop for a quick coffee, grab a magazine, and make it to the gate with plenty of time to board the plane.

But then again, when does life ever go "according to plan"?

Tick Tock

I check my watch. OK, who am I kidding? I haven't worn a watch in years. I scramble to find my cell phone to check the time when I realize my jeans . . . my favorite jeans . . . are still not dry! Girls, you know you can't put jeans in a dryer and expect them to fit, right? So, I choose to air-dry my denim—which, by the way, is very hard to time. So now with less than two hours until takeoff I'm forced, let me repeat myself, *forced,* to put my favorite jeans into the dryer. So now, I wait, staring at the machine as the jeans flip and spin inside the cylinder—willing it to hurry. I time the tapping of my feet with the little clanking sound the button makes as metal hits metal. *Clomp.* Pause. *Clomp.* Pause. *Clomp.* Pause. Pause. *Clomp.*

Six minutes later they are past the damp stage and on their way to warm when I decide I can't wait any longer and shove the half-dry denim into my suitcase. Good. Still enough time to make the twenty-two-minute drive from my house to the airport. Do I still have time for my stops? Yes! This small victory is celebrated with a little dance as I throw my luggage into the back of the car.

Two minutes into my airport drive it begins to rain. And in *my* city, rain is a traffic-stopping event. Suddenly, drivers have no idea what to do when the strange liquid starts to splatter against their windshields. What is this dewy substance that falls from yonder sky? Bewildered, traffic slows to a crawl. And precious minutes tick by as I wait to get on the freeway. Waiting. But I'm still cool. Not frustrated . . . yet.

Then I have a brilliant idea . . . take the tollway! Sure, it costs money, but it is faster and in the rain I need to make up the time. I think I've made a wise maneuver in choosing my route until I realize that I am not alone in my brilliance. It seems others have the same idea. As I pull onto the tollway I see taillights for days. I tell myself, *Be patient. You'll get there on time.*

But after I wait *twelve minutes* at the first tollbooth—do you know how long twelve minutes can feel when it is raining and you are late for the airport? I am beginning to get a tiny bit frustrated. It seems that rain not only decreases driving speed in my city but coin-tossing swiftness as well. With each passing minute I say good-bye to my much-needed coffee stop and know I will be foregoing any fun magazine purchase for this trip.

With exactly thirty-three minutes before takeoff, I pull into the parking garage at the airport. Forget the cheap parking lot with the shuttle. I have to go the high-dollar route and park at the terminal. I circle up and up and up to the top of the garage, locate a spot, yank my roller bag out, and run—full sprint—for the terminal check-in.

Panting, I burst through the doors and hurry past the baggage check-in area and go straight to security . . . where, you guessed it, I wait in line for four minutes as the kind, extremely detailed, and meticulous ID/boarding pass patrol woman thoroughly examines each person's identity and flight credentials. I'm smiling. (Fake smiling. Like I'd just lost *American Idol* and am pretending to be happy for the winner.) "Thank you. Yes, you have a good day too."

Shuffle. Stop. Shuffle. Stop. There are six, yes I counted, six X-ray machines, but there is only one in operation this afternoon. Finally, I shuffle up to the machine only to wait for the sweet old man in front of me to take off his shoes (lace-ups, by the way) and put them neatly on the conveyor belt. The gray plastic bins are all stuck together, so this process takes a while.

My turn arrives and I unload my suitcase, briefcase, laptop (it must have its own little carrier), and my purse onto the X-ray machine. Barefoot, I cross through the beeper machine and wait at the end of the conveyor for my belongings. Waiting. Waiting. Missing my plane. Missing my plane. *Tick, tock. Tick, tock.* Waiting some more, when I hear, "Miss, is this your stuff?"

Uhhhhhhhhh. Fake smile.

The kind federal officer then asks me to step aside as he unzips my carry-on bag. Girls, feel my pain as I tell you that in my haste I forgot all about the plastic bag rule (something about three ounces and a sandwich bag making the world a safer place). And do you know what this man is about to throw away? He proceeds without a moment's hesitation or guilt to toss my shampoo, face cleanser, moisturizer, lip gloss, and mascara. MASCARA! I want someone to tell me how my favorite mascara is a threat to national security!

I didn't care if I was missing my plane anymore. This was a tragedy. I quickly calculated the cost of his heartless deed and surmised it was a good thing I didn't have the time for my other airport purchases. My money clearly needed to go to a greater cause—beauty. Plus, the time I spent waiting on Mr. No Respect for Beauty Products to clear me through security—I'd probably missed my flight.

Oh, but I hadn't!

No, ladies, my plane, which was now due to take off in six minutes, wasn't even in the city. Yes, that's right, I rushed and ran myself ragged to get there only to sprint up to the gate, haggard and mascara-less, to see the news in flashing capital letters—FLIGHT DELAYED! You've got to be kidding me— more waiting? The friendly, yet annoyed, airline staffer informs the waiting passengers that our plane and flight crew are in another city, and she will need us to wait patiently for them to be redirected.

Wait patiently? Do these two words even belong in the same sentence? It is beginning to dawn on me that God might be try- ing to teach me something. A good two-and-a-half hours later our plane arrives, and the awaiting passengers herd around the gate like horses waiting for feed as they quickly prepare the plane. Now, three hours after our scheduled departure, they finally call for boarding. At last! I'm on my way.

Silly girl. What was I thinking?

Sure, we do finally board, but only to sit on the tarmac for another forty-four minutes before takeoff. Something about the rain?

It's an epidemic.

THREE HOURS LATER, I finally land in Los Angeles. My friend who is meeting me there is also waiting for me at the airport. I soooooooo feel her pain. Elected to go get the rental car, I schlep my belongings onto the shuttle and arrive to find myself in the longest line in rental car history. I almost walked out. It was just too much. I was exhausted simply from waiting all day.

Seriously, I was at my waiting threshold when the humor of it all slowly soaked in. I kid you not, as I stood in line (for over an hour) waiting for our car, playing on the piped-in music system was none other than "Waiting for the World to Change."

At that point I just laughed out loud—it seems that God has a sense of humor and was obviously trying to teach me something about waiting.

While experiences like these can be frustrating—a true test of patience—they are not a wilderness. A wilderness of waiting has nothing to do with traffic, nor does it have anything to do with standing in line. A wilderness of waiting is about one thing: living with an unmet desire. And the big difference between the waiting I've described and a wilderness is this: even while waiting in the longest line, you know eventually it will be your turn. But when waiting on an unmet desire . . . you don't have that security or assurance. There is the added element of the unknown. A major question looms—will my life always be this way? That question can be torture. That's why I call waiting a wilderness.

Polar Bear Attacks

To desire is to long for something. To hope, dream, or yearn. A wilderness of unmet desire is waiting for that hope to become a reality. It is the postponement of a longing of your soul. The feeling that your life is standing still while others' appear to be moving in high speed. A woman in this wilderness may ask herself, "Did God push 'pause' on my life and forget to inform me?"

Let me ask you a hard question. What are *you* waiting for? Mr. Right?

Or, are you a woman who is waiting for God to change your Mr. Right?

Is your unmet desire simply to feel loved?

Perhaps you are like many women I know who live with the longing for children.

Or, are you the mother who is waiting for God to change the child you already have?

An unmet desire can be financial, relational, or physical.

What is the unmet desire of your heart? What is that secret longing that keeps you asking God the question, *When?*

"I think I'm waiting for my life to begin," a friend replied when I asked her, "What are you waiting for?" Reading her e-mail, I could feel the disappointment in her words. Her response wasn't flippant . . . these are the sincere words of a girl who feels she has been left stranded in the wilderness of unmet desire. You see, my friend is single and in her thirties. And do you know the urban myth about single women in their thirties? Something about lighting striking or polar bears attacking being more likely than marriage? What a cruel myth! (Please tell me this is a myth, right?)

I digress. So sorry. Back to my point: My friend desires children, but with no prospect of a husband on the horizon, for that desire she, too, must wait. Meanwhile most of her friends are now married and raising kids, and it seems God remembered them but for some reason He forgot her. When having a family is the biggest desire of your heart, then it does seem like you are "waiting on life to begin" if that dream is not yet a reality.

What are *you* waiting for?

Perhaps you are reading this and you don't relate to the desire for a family just yet, but you do know the pain of loneliness. For you, it may simply be the desire for a good friendship. Or maybe you are not in a hurry to get married, but you wouldn't complain at all if God decided to bring along a date every now and then.

Or maybe you can relate to another girlfriend of mine. She is married, but for years she has struggled with infertility. Today she is waiting to hear from the doctor if she is finally pregnant. The longing to be a mother is physical, and she faces each new birth announcement and baby shower invitation that comes in the mail with the same thought: *When will it be my turn?*

What are you waiting for?

I know plenty of women who are waiting for that one specific prayer to be answered—the prayer for a loved one's salvation or for healing from an illness. Or maybe your unmet desire deals more with your calling. You desire to use your gifts and talents in a meaningful way, but today you feel useless.

Are you waiting for God to open a door?

For provision?

For direction?

What are you waiting for?

Are you asking God, "When will it be my turn?"

Living with an unmet desire can be at times painful, but waiting can also be a huge blessing in our lives if we learn how to wait. Yet in our instant-gratification culture, we don't like to wait nor do we know how. So . . . what's a girl to do? First, let's examine the dangers a woman faces in this wilderness, and then we will learn the secret to living with an unmet desire.

Danger!

Horseback riding is one of my passions. There is nothing like galloping through an open field to refresh the soul.

This past weekend I traded in my new summer wedges for my cowboy boots as my family and I saddled up the horses and spent the afternoon riding through the woods of the Texas river country. A few hours into the ride, we happened upon a small creek. The water appeared to be shallow enough for the horses to cross with ease. This theory proved to be true as each of us filed through the creek—that is until the last horse attempted to cross.

The last horse, Rosie, a sweet-tempered mare, cautiously stepped hoof by hoof into the stream. Then as she placed her left leg a little farther into the water, her whole body fell in. Unknown to us, that part of the creek was a five-foot drop, and both horse and rider were in for a bath. Thankfully, the horse is fine. (Although my brother's pride is still a little sore.) The lesson? Dangerous pitfalls can happen whenever we least expect them.

Danger #1 Envy

Envy. Green is not my color. But I'll be honest, in the wilderness one of Satan's seductive ploys is to spark that oh-so-green-with-envy feeling in a woman's heart. How? By zeroing in on the "have-nots." He calls into question the goodness of God. Why would God make her wait for something she desires so badly? Let's recap. This tactic goes back to Satan's ultimate plan and purpose: to rob God of our worship and to destroy our faith in Him. So, what better way to burn fellowship than by convincing a girl that God wants "good" for everyone else but her.

You know how they say timing is everything? Well, my best friend's wedding landed right smack in the middle of the hardest days of *the incident* (my breakup and rejection trauma). And everyone else within a fifty-mile radius seemed to get the wedding itch about that time too. Those months, the wedding season, were a constant reminder of the "have-not" in my life. Each bridesmaid dress I bought, each blender purchased, and every bridal shower attended was an opportunity for the Enemy to make another little stab and say, *God forgot you*.

Thankfully, I recognized this danger from a distance and was able to sidestep disaster with careful preparation. Prayerfully, I asked God to help me celebrate other people's joy in the midst of my sorrow. I knew if I indulged in envy then I would be in a far worse situation. God answered this prayer in a supernatural way. Throughout the darkest days of grief and battles with rejection, God gave me a true joy for others that was inexplicable. I'll never forget going with my best friend to buy her wedding dress. My heart was hemorrhaging, but the experience was so beautiful. We laughed, we cried, and she twirled around like a princess, and all the while God protected me from envy.

I loved every minute of it. There was one moment when I caught my reflection in a mirror, and I saw that I was smiling from ear to ear as I watched her parade dresses in front of us. I was shocked by my own joy and thought, *This is so Jesus*.

Realizing envy was a danger in the wilderness prepared me to pray for my own protection. I asked God for a special grace so that I could be truly excited for others in the midst of my own pain. I pass on this advice to you. Ask God to fill you with His love and joy for others. Ask Him to protect you from the taunts of the Enemy and to guard your mind from comparing and coveting. I can't take one ounce of credit for what God did in my heart. But I can give Him glory for doing what I could not have done in my own capacity—giving me the ability to celebrate and not to envy. Looking back, I realize that the daily dose of joy was my "manna" in the wilderness. God provided something I didn't have on my own, and through it He proved His faithfulness.

Danger #2 Manipulation

No one likes to wait. The next time you find yourself delayed in traffic, check out your emotional response and that of those around you. You'll see what I mean. What is the gut reaction of most people when faced with a life delay? Fix it. Find an alternate route. Yet in a wilderness of unmet desire one of the biggest temptations women will face is the urge to take control and change their situation. This temptation can spell disaster.

Just recently I recognized this danger (and my pathetic lack of patience) when faced with a major traffic jam in the city. I was rushing to dinner with a friend when I turned toward the freeway, only to discover that every other person in the tristate area was heading in the same direction. After asking myself if there was a hurricane evacuation that I'd ignored, I then reasoned it was just a typical day of construction chaos. Always the clever navigator, I quickly devised a new route to my destination. The only problem was that my new route was a construction zone covered in a good layer of mud.

Imagine this scene with me . . . sitting in my freshly washed SUV on a congested feeder road, I stare longingly at what appears to be an easy shortcut to my desired destination. If successful, it would save me an hour wait. I ponder . . . do I attempt the shortcut . . . or not? A quick decision was needed; the cars lining up behind me weren't too fond of my indecision.

Urged forward by my increasing impatience, I go for it. Maneuvering my vehicle toward the muddy crossover, I make a beeline for my destination. Actually, bees would be embarrassed by the slow pace. No lie. As soon as my tires hit the "shortcut," I began skidding and sliding, and within three seconds my four-wheel-drive SUV was stuck in two feet of mud. Stuck!!! Seriously, my car, which was purchased for just such maneuvers, was wheel-locked in some pretty impressive Texas mud.

Girls, it took me more than an hour to get my car removed from the mess. At one point I had to get out and physically push my now-filthy car back and forth to unlodge it. (PS: the image is not complete unless you understand I was wearing a dress and high heels.) Now, I'm really late . . . and filthy.

Why all the mess? Simply because I didn't want to wait. Instead, I chose to take matters into my own hands and "devise a plan." I wonder: How many girls out there can relate to this scenario? How many women grew tired of living with an unmet desire and manipulated a way to fulfill that longing? Countless tales could be told of the "mess" that manipulation brings.

- Did you grow tired of waiting on God to bring Mr. Right and now you are stuck with Mr. Right Now?
- Did you manipulate a situation to get "your way" and now you are living with the consequences of that decision?
- What "shortcut" to meeting the desire of your heart are you considering? What are the potential costs of not waiting upon the Lord?

I ask these questions because I know that in the wilderness of unmet desire there are times when our hearts scream for an easy way out. We don't like to wait. Especially when waiting

114

turns into a wilderness, we are in danger of falling headfirst into the pit of manipulation.

Danger #3 Worry

The other danger lurking in the wilderness of waiting is that of worry. Most women deal with worry and anxiety at some level. But when it is future oriented (What will happen if I never have . . . ?), then anxiety causes restlessness and unnecessary emotional turmoil. Worry and fear go hand in hand. These fearful emotions ultimately say, "I don't trust God to meet my heart's desire."

When I think about the danger of worry, the image of quicksand comes to mind. How many times have you watched a movie where the hero bogs down into a pit of quicksand, only to be saved at the last minute by grabbing a nearby tree branch and pulling herself out? Depicted as a living creature, quicksand can suck a woman down into a bottomless pit, never to be heard from again.

Worry and quicksand have heaps in common. For the persons trapped in quicksand, panic tends to get them in trouble. When they panic they flail about and become more and more trapped by the sand. Likewise, when we become consumed with worry, we tend to flail about emotionally and cause ourselves to get into a far worse situation. I know tons of women who live without peace and joy because they allow worry to consume them. Instead of enjoying the present, they live in dread of the future and allow their thinking to be controlled by the question, "What if God never provides the desire of my heart?" These women desperately need to grab hold of something solid to pull them out of the pit of worry.

So . . . what's a girl to do? When in the wilderness of unmet desire, what is the right way to wait so that we don't fall into the dangers of envy, manipulation, and worry? If there is any person in Scripture who knows a thing or two about waiting, it is King David. As a teenager, David received a promise that he would be the next king over Israel. But it would be nearly two decades before that promise was fulfilled. Did God lie? Did God forget? No! God had a definite purpose in the wait. Throughout the Psalms (most of which were written by David), he teaches us some incredible truths about waiting in the wilderness of unmet desire.

When David was a young man, God sent the prophet Samuel to his father's house to choose David out of all of his brothers to be the future king of Israel. God described him as "a man after his own heart" (1 Sam. 13:14 NIV). What a bright future lay ahead of this young man! He was the chosen one. David loved the Lord, and he deeply desired to fulfill his calling to be king. Yet it was twenty years before David's desire and God's promise was fulfilled. Like you and I, David entered a wilderness—a wilderness of unmet desire. In this wilderness, he, too, faced the same dangers I've described: envy, manipulation, and worry.

Yet through David's experience we learn a powerful lesson about waiting. Come with me now into the wilderness region of Israel where David is hiding out . . . literally. It is in these wilds that we see David face the giants of envy, manipulation, and worry, which he is no longer able to slay with a mere pebble and slingshot. This is truly treacherous territory and will require a whole new set of skills.

A King in Waiting

David is a wanted man with a high price on his head. So, how did David find himself in this situation? I'm sure if you were to have asked him, he would've said, "Well certainly not hiding in a cave, hunted like an animal while I wait for God to remove Saul, the current king of Israel, that's for sure. This wilderness thing was sure not MY plan." Looking at David's story, we learn our first lesson for the wilderness of waiting. Here's how it is told in Scripture: "David left Gath and took refuge in the cave of Adullam. When David's brothers and his father's whole family heard, they went down and joined him there. In addition, every man who was desperate, in debt, or discontented rallied around him, and he became their leader. About 400 men were with him" (1 Sam. 22:1–2).

So we see that King Saul pursued David throughout Israel. David fled into the wilderness because Saul, in a jealous rage, decided to kill him. David hid and waited in a cave in the wilderness. Meanwhile, hundreds joined him there . . . and they, too, waited on God to change the situation in the land. The first lesson we learn from David is this: we are not alone. Those with him in that cave were waiting just as he was.

Girls, we are so guilty of comparison—of looking at other people's lives and thinking that they have it "perfect" or "easy." When we choose to compare, our thoughts lead us to host our very own pity party.

Like David, we are not alone. The question is not *if* we are waiting but *how* we are waiting. Most people have unmet desires. When we forget this truth, we tend to feel sorry for ourselves and send out the invites to our pity party. And do we ever have help in planning this party? Satan loves to throw this shindig . . . it is his specialty. He knows that if he can get us to wallow in self-pity, then he can do great damage to our faith. He begins with his subtle accusations and then increases his attack by glamorizing the lives of everyone else:

Everyone else has it easy.

Your friend doesn't have to wait.

You are the only one living with an unmet desire.

Poor you.

Please recognize his motive: not only does Satan seek to undermine a woman's faith and trust in God, but he also desires to plant seeds of jealousy within a woman's heart that will grow into hate and bitterness toward God and others.

Left-Handed Shame

I kept my left hand in my lap all night. Not out of polite social etiquette that says keeping one's left hand daintily on your napkin while dining is proper. No, my left hand remained in my lap simply because I didn't want it to feel . . . how I should say . . . left out. You see, mine was the only left hand at this dinner party for fourteen women that was missing a wedding ring. I really felt sorry for my left hand. I didn't realize it was the odd one at first, but after hearing the conversation to my left that was about breast pumps and the conversation to my right that was about which neighborhood afforded the better school district, it dawned on me: *I am now a single woman in a married woman's world. When did this happen?*

All of these women, at one time or another, were single. While a couple, I think, did get married in high school, the rest were at one point my single girlfriends. They've graduated. And here I am . . . me and my left hand.

Freeze. This is the makings of a pity party. Ingredients: mix one single woman reeling from a breakup and thirteen married women, and you've got yourself one fine fiesta. Thankfully, this birthday party didn't end in a pity party. Instead, this night provided me with a powerful truth: I am not alone in the wait.

As I tuned out the whispers of the Enemy and stopped thinking about myself for half a second, I listened to the women around me, and I realized something: each woman had an unmet desire in her heart. I was not alone.

- One woman mentioned feeling all alone at home with her kids and longed for genuine friendship again.
- Another was waiting to lose the "baby weight" she had put on and was beginning to lose hope that it would ever change.
- Others were married but still waiting for God to provide them with children.
- One girlfriend desired to be reconciled with a family member.

Everyone has "their thing." Not that I desire others to be miserable, that is not what I'm saying, but having company during the waiting takes the edge off of the awkward feeling of "it's just me out here in these crazy woods."

This week one of my best girlfriends phoned. She lives in Australia, so we have to schedule our chitchats for times when we are both in waking hours. When we do get to talk, we go deep—no small talk. I was relating to her the content of this chapter and some of the difficulty I'd been having in writing about the wilderness of unmet desire, given the fact that I was still living in it. I said, "Writing about rejection is not so tough because I'm not living in it anymore. The same goes for despair and temptation, but this one—I'm still smack-dab in the middle of it."

She paused for a minute and said, "I hear ya . . . that's a tough one. But I read a book the other day, and the author said something that really stuck with me. This writer said, 'Marriage doesn't make you happy; it just makes you married.'"

I replied, "That is so true . . . that's pretty good stuff."

She laughed out loud and said, "Marian, *you* wrote that."

There's nothing like having someone quote you . . . to you. I felt very small. But she was right. During this past year of grief (heartbreak, rejection, and the countless other emotions that I've experienced), I allowed myself to forget a fundamental truth—one that my entire first book, *Sex and the City Uncovered,* was based upon: The only love that will fill a woman's soul is the love of Jesus Christ.

Somewhere in the wilderness of unmet desire, as I continue to wait for God to provide marriage, I think I had allowed marriage to become this sort of Holy Grail that I needed to attain in order to be happy. Or worse, I was allowing the institution itself to be the measure of my worth. If I'm not married, does that mean I'm not as good as the other girls who are? Does my singleness reflect a lack in my relationship with God?

I'm so glad my friend called me out on my inconsistency. I love truth, and I especially love friends who will speak truth to me. Today, like David, I'm still waiting, but I'm doing so with a different mind-set. Speaking of David, he also faced the second big danger while waiting in the wilderness of unmet desire: manipulation.

While David and his men are hiding in the caves in the wilderness, he has the perfect opportunity to dethrone Saul and take the kingdom of Israel for himself. This scene could be straight out of an action-thriller movie:

> When Saul came back after dealing with the Philistines, he was told, "David is now in the wilderness of En Gedi." Saul took three companies—the best he could find in all Israel—and set out in search of David and his men in the region of Wild Goat Rocks. He came to some sheep pens along the road. There was a cave there and Saul went in to relieve himself. David and his men were huddled far back in the same cave. David's men whispered to him, "Can you believe it? This is the day GOD was talking about when he said, 'I'll put your enemy in your hands. You can do whatever you want with him.'" Quiet as a cat, David crept up and cut off a piece of Saul's royal robe. (1 Sam. 24:1–4 MSG)

What a tempting opportunity David faces! He can so easily take matters into his own hands and physically remove Saul from the throne. Who would blame him? After all, his friends are encouraging him to do so. But is this God's best? Is murder the way God would have him come to power? Nudged by the conviction of the Holy Spirit, David realizes manipulation is a sin:

> Immediately, he felt guilty. He said to his men, "GOD forbid that I should have done this to my master, GOD's anointed, that I should so much as raise a finger against him. He's GOD's anointed!" David held his men in check with these words and wouldn't let them pounce on Saul. Saul got up, left the cave, and went on down the road.

Then David stood at the mouth of the cave and
called to Saul, "My master! My king!" Saul looked
back. David fell to his knees and bowed in reverence.
He called out, "Why do you listen to those who say
'David is out to get you'? This very day with your very
own eyes you have seen that just now in the cave GOD
put you in my hands. My men wanted me to kill you,
but I wouldn't do it. I told them that I won't lift a finger against my master—he's GOD's anointed. Oh, my
father, look at this, look at this piece that I cut from
your robe. I could have cut you—killed you!—but I
didn't. Look at the evidence! I'm not against you. I'm
no rebel. I haven't sinned against you, and yet you're
hunting me down to kill me. Let's decide which of
us is in the right. GOD may avenge me, but it is in his
hands, not mine." (1 Sam. 24:5–12 MSG)

David stares manipulation straight in the eyes and says no.
In that moment he chooses to trust God, to wait upon the Lord,
to let God be God and decide when and how his desire to be
king would be fulfilled. And in his right response he proves he
is after all a "man after God's own heart."

When David had finished saying all this, Saul said,
"Can this be the voice of my son David?" and he wept
in loud sobs. "You're the one in the right, not me," he
continued. "You've heaped good on me; I've dumped
evil on you. And now you've done it again—treated
me generously. GOD put me in your hands and you
didn't kill me. Why? When a man meets his enemy,
does he send him down the road with a blessing? May
GOD give you a bonus of blessings for what you've

done for me today! I know now beyond doubt that
you will rule as king. The kingdom of Israel is already
in your grasp!" (1 Sam. 24:16–20 MSG)

Like David, we will face many too-good-to-be-true oppor-
tunities while waiting in the wilderness of unmet desire. My
suggestion is: before acting on any impulses, check with God.
Read His Word. Go to Him in prayer and ask Him if *your* plan is
His plan. If your plan contradicts God's revealed will (e.g., murder, manipulation, or misappropriation of funds), then we can
be pretty certain that God is not the one leading you to act.

Now that I'm back in the dating world again, I've heard that
my standards for what I want in my husband are too high. I'm
often encouraged to simply settle for a little less than God's best
or, even worse, to ignore God's will when it comes to whom I
should date and marry. (As if "till death do us part" was only a
short season. PLEASE!!!) This type of advice is dangerous and
can lead to horrible life choices. The lesson I learn from King
David is this: God is good, and He can and will meet the desires
of my heart in His timing . . . not mine. My only responsibility
is to let God be God.

So, please consider this a public notice. I'm not interested
in any of the following setups (and no, girls, it really doesn't
matter how cute or tall he may be):

- I will not date your best friend's brother-in-law who's
  not a Christian but reportedly had a "spiritual" experience in Tibet last year.
- I will not date your hairdresser who may like girls . . .
  but you're not so sure.
- I will not date your coworker who is still married . . .
  but you're pretty sure that's not working out.

I appreciate the well-meaning sentiments, but I'll wait for God's best.

Waiting without Worry

So far we've examined how in the wilderness of unmet desires women confront two dangerous hazards—envy and manipulation. But the biggest danger still needs addressing, and this is the bad boy called "worry."

Worry is wretched. In Psalm 37, David (a man who knows a thing or two about the subject) teaches us the secret to waiting in the wilderness of unmet desire without falling into the pit of worry. I highly suggest you take the time to read the entire psalm; it is worth putting to memory, but for our purposes we are going to look at four verses—perhaps the most well-known four:

> Delight yourself in the LORD;
> And He will give you the desires of your heart.
> Commit your way to the LORD,
> Trust also in Him, and He will do it.
> He will bring forth your righteousness as the light
> And your judgment as the noonday.
> Rest in the LORD and wait patiently for Him.
>
> (Ps. 37:4–7 NASB)

If you are like me, you read this verse and a big question comes to mind: what does it mean to "delight [myself] *in* the LORD"? I've mulled that phrase over and over again in the past few weeks. Selfishly, I want to conquer this command because I want my desires to be met. It's like God is a math professor who has given us a cheat sheet for the final exam so that we can write out the formula: Delight = Desires.

But this delight thing is not so simple. As I've pondered this truth more and more, I've come to realize the deep connection between my delight and my desire. How the two are often hand and glove.

Just yesterday, I was on the phone with my friend's mom. In the midst of our conversation, she dropped the delight word. I'll give you a little context so you'll get her meaning. We were talking about her granddaughter, and she said, "I desired for many years to be a grandmother, and it is the delight of my life to be with that child." A lightbulb went off in my head, and the definition for delight that I'd been searching for flashed before me in living color. As she went on and on about her love for this child, I got it. Delight means to enjoy. Delight means to long to be near the object of one's delight. Delight means to be consumed with the life of another. As she spoke of the pleasure she found in Lillian's smile and the sheer joy of experiencing life with her, I realized what the Lord wanted of me when He said, "Delight yourself *in* the LORD."

Jesus wants my affection.

Jesus wants me to enjoy His presence.

Jesus desires my heart to be captivated with His glory and beauty.

Then I asked myself a tough question: Is Jesus my delight?

There have been seasons in my life when I could say without a doubt that the delight of my life was my Lord and Savior Jesus Christ. The deepest passion of my soul was to be in His presence and the longing of my heart to simply hear His voice and witness His power. But there have been other times that the delight in my life has shifted to something or someone far less worthy of my affection and attention. I had a season where a guy stole my heart and he became my delight. Just recently I realized how pathetic my affections can be when I understood that my work was eclipsing my love for Jesus. But there is only One—and will always be only One—who is the truest object of our desire and that is our Creator, Jesus Christ. In the Bible we are told we are created by Him and for Him. That being said, then it would make the most sense that we are only fully alive when we are fully delighting in Him.

I will never read Psalm 37 without thinking of my thirtieth birthday. That weekend my roommate and I flew down to Cozumel, Mexico. I wanted to escape to the beach for a few days to celebrate my birthday and to get some much-needed rest. It was there that the Lord taught me the correlation between delight and desire.

Delight and Desire

It was still pitch-black outside, yet I was wide awake. Throwing back the covers, I scrounged for my sandals and my Bible and then fumbled my way out of the hotel room toward the beach. I love the ocean, and that morning I was guided as much by the sound of the waves crashing as I was by the first glimmer of light breaking at the horizon.

You see, friends, I felt called. For some reason I had to experience this sunrise. A deep desire in my soul propelled me toward the breaking light.

Not being a morning person, I thought it was strange that I would be wide awake at 5:00 a.m. while on vacation. Yet, when awakened an hour before dawn and unable to go back to sleep, I sensed God had awakened me to meet with Him.

Nearing the beach, I increased my speed to a jog so that I would be at the shore by first light. I arrived on the sand just in time to see radiant colors burst along the horizon and dispel the haze of darkness. It was glorious. Rays of light ushered in a new day. I watched and waited, simply enjoying the beauty God created before my eyes.

Drinking in this beauty, I felt God's presence. I began to pray—quiet words of thankfulness and praises to the Lord for all that He has done. Most of all, I simply enjoyed being in His presence. This moment defined delight.

Basking in God's glory, I opened my Bible. Turning to Psalm 37:4, I began reading the familiar words, "Delight yourself in the LORD and he will give you the desires of you heart" (NIV). Somehow I knew that this was one of those rare moments of pure delight: peace, beauty, calm, glory. Experiencing the creation with my Creator, my heart burst from the simple joy of it all.

After reading the first part of the passage, I paused and was about to move on when I sensed the Lord asking me this question: "Marian, what do you desire?"

Right there, with sand scrunched between my toes and the warm Caribbean wind blowing through my hair, I had a very "nonfilter moment" with Jesus. (You know, when you say something before you really have time to formulate the "proper" response?) With my internal editor still asleep back in the hotel room, I spoke freely and without hesitation to the Object of my delight. My response was very telling, and I said, "Do You really care?"

Astounded by my own frankness, the magic of the moment came to a screeching halt. I thought to myself, *Wow, can I say that to God? I think I just did.* Honestly, I had no idea I felt that way. It seems God brought me to the beach that morning not only to reveal His glory by dispelling the darkness through a beautiful sunrise but also to dispel a lie that was in my heart about His heart for me.

Somewhere deep within I believed the lie that God didn't really care about my desires. I knew He wanted good for other people, but I didn't quite believe it for myself. As I heard my own response to His question, I began to cry and let my walls of self-protection fall down. God was showing me that I'd stopped desiring because I really didn't believe that He cared about the desires of *my* heart.

And then with a fatherly love He asked me again, "Marian, what do *you* desire?"

As I analyzed my previous response, I realized my heart questioned the goodness of God.

Does God really care about me?

Does God really want good for me?

Does God really care about the unmet desires in my heart?

I knew in my head that the answer to my questions was, "yes, *yes,* and YES." But my silly heart didn't believe it, or it was just too afraid to believe.

The Lord asked me *what* I desired because for years I'd coped with my unmet desires by simply pretending they didn't exist. In other words . . . denial. But the not-so-funny thing was this: my desires were still there. Covered under walls of self-protection and plastic platitudes of piety, my heart still desired—deeply desired—things that only God fully knew. So on that morning, which so perfectly captured the meaning of delight, my God asked me to commit to Him my desires.

PS—*that* is the next verse: "Commit your way to the LORD; trust in him and he will do this" (Ps. 37:5 NIV). There, on the white sand, God wanted me to lay before Him my heart. Lay it bare. Pull down the plastic covering and get real and stop denying that I had unmet desires and risk living with the longing.

The word *commit* means to hand something over. So instead of hiding my heart's desires away and pretending they didn't exist, God was calling me to bring them out into the open of our relationship and entrust them to Him.

There, on the beach in the midst of early-morning joggers and yoga posers, I did an exercise of my own—I committed the desires of my heart to the Lord. Looking back, I am amazed at how, in the short time since that vacation, God has met and exceeded so many of the things I asked of Him that day: prayers for personal wholeness and healing, prayers for ministry and calling, and prayers for friendships and love. Of course, there are still the "unmets," but that is the journey of waiting and walking with the Lord that we all go through in this life.

The question that remains is *how* do we live with these unmet desires? How do we live with our longings without being emotionally tortured by the "have not" and without falling headfirst into the pit of worry? Funny we should ask. For in verse 7, David teaches us the secret to waiting without worry. The secret? *"Rest in the LORD and wait patiently for Him"* (NASB).

If I can be oh-so-scholarly for just a minute, I think that what this means in the original language of the Bible is to "chill out, girlfriend." David goes on to say this multiple times in Psalm 37 when he reminds us to "fret not." I love that! I know when a woman is in a wilderness season she can do some serious fretting.

When, God?

Why, God?

How, God?

But the Bible says to us, "Stop all your fretting, sister girl . . . God is still running the universe, He knows what He is doing, and He doesn't need your help." Or as my dad loves to remind me all the time, "Marian . . . God is not taking Maalox over your situation." So, what does David teach us about the wilderness of unmet desire? Rest and wait. I like the simplicity of this wilderness skill. We can relax because God is not confused or frazzled about how His plan for our lives will be accomplished.

It's a Wonderful Life!

It was the night before Christmas (and all through the house . . . just kidding, I couldn't help myself) when I fell asleep while watching a movie. I must confess that I have my own little Christmas Eve tradition when home at my parents' house. Long after the board games are put away and the final gifts are wrapped and placed under the tree, I plop myself on the couch to watch my favorite holiday flick, *It's a Wonderful Life!*

It is tragic if you have not seen this movie. Because we are friends, I will ignore this lapse in judgment, but you must promise me that you will not let this next Christmas season go by without watching it. Trust me, it is worth it. So for those of you who haven't seen the movie, let me give you a quick trailer.

The film takes place in the fictional town of Bedford Falls shortly after World War II and stars Jimmy Stewart as George Bailey, a man whose attempted suicide on Christmas Eve gains the attention of a guardian angel, Clarence, who is sent to help him in his hour of need. Most of the film is told through flashbacks spanning George's entire life and is narrated by unseen angels who are preparing Clarence for his mission to save George. Through these flashbacks we see all the people whose lives have been touched by George and the difference he has made to the community in which he lives.

Ironically, George Bailey is a man who walked through the wilderness of unmet desire. He longed for a life of adventure; he desired to travel and see the world. Yet George's life was confined to Bedford Falls, and he never did stretch his wings and fly away. I love the last scene of this movie, in which George discovers his life is not one of disappointment but rather divine appointment. Surrounded by his family and friends, George Bailey realizes it is a really good thing that life didn't go according to *his* plan. For there was a better plan for George Bailey, and it took an angel in need of wings to reveal this truth to him.

A few years ago during my Christmas tradition, I drifted off to sleep somewhere after George Bailey crashed his car. But I wasn't asleep long before I was awakened by a noise. Once awake I realized it was the sound of burglars breaking into our house! No, I wasn't dreaming about the Grinch; these were real-life robbers sneaking in to steal Christmas presents.

Wide-eyed and frightened, I jumped off the couch and did the only thing this Texas girl knew to do in a situation like this. I yelled, "Daddy, get the gun!"

Those four words sent those two would-be present bandits running for the county line. It seems my dad's gun collection is infamous to more than just my ex-boyfriends. So when I yelled for armed backup, the robbers bolted out the door.

Over an hour later, after the police came and went, and the tree was double-checked for missing trinkets, I found myself back on the couch where the whole ordeal began. Wrapped in a blanket and watching George Bailey discover . . . it *is* a wonderful life.

There was absolutely no way I was going to fall asleep after that ordeal. My heart was pounding so loudly I could hear the thud. And then my imagination began to take over, and I played through my mind all of the "what ifs" of the evening. I needed to rest, but I was too wound up and freaked out to get any shut-eye.

I stared at the TV for another ten minutes before I heard the sound of Dad walking through the house. His walk is unmistakable. A small man he is not, so when he is coming—you know it. Dad came in the family room where I was watching TV and took a seat in *his* chair.

There is something about Dad's presence. Almost instantly, I lowered my head onto the sofa cushion and watched as Bedford Falls celebrated George's return home and the saving of the old Building and Loan. It is one of my favorite moments in movie history. I especially enjoyed the sweetness of it this night. For that scene says, "Everything is going to be OK."

And something in my heart felt that was the case. For when

my dad entered the room and sat in *his* chair, my worried heart ceased its fretting and my breathing returned to the slow, deep breaths of the weary. Within minutes I was fast asleep.

Reflecting on that night I know there was a deep connection between my ability to rest and my belief. I knew without a shadow of a doubt that with my father in the room I was completely safe. Nothing and no one would harm me. My confidence in that truth told my worried heart to "fret not" and my anxious mind to fear not—all would be just fine. And this girl went fast to sleep.

Living with unmet desires is much the same. It's so easy to get wound up with the "what ifs" of the future. When we let ourselves go there and dwell in worry, life becomes miserable. I truly believe the lesson of Psalm 37 is this: chill out. When we start believing that God does care about our hearts and He still knows how to run the universe, then we can stop our fretting and rest. I know I, too, will have a "wonderful life" because my heavenly Father sits on *His* chair—which just happens to be His throne in heaven.

Looking back over the wilderness season, I can honestly say the area I've changed the most is this: I am a woman at rest. God has so proven His faithfulness that I am far less likely to worry and fret about my unmet desires or the unknown future. What's changed? I know God's "no" in my past was the best thing that ever happened to me. As a result, I trust Him even more with my future. I rest, believing God's plan is far better than my plan. While His way may not align with my way or come to pass on my timetable, I can cease fretting because I know God is good. I know He is in control. And most important, I know I can trust Him.

part 2

chapter 8

Wilderness Skills

Bear attacks are rare,
but whenever you come across a bear,
it's very important not to run,
no matter how scared you may be.
Running may prompt a bear to give chase,
and you cannot outrun a bear.

—NEW MEXICO DEPARTMENT OF GAME AND FISH

FACT: Bears can climb trees faster than they can run.
—DWIGHT, *THE OFFICE*

I'm not a girl who is prone to reading instructions.

This character flaw proved to be detrimental in school. Teachers are oh so picky about "doing it their way." Time and again, I would put my debate skills to use in pointing out, "There is more than one way to solve a problem." Alas, with eye rolls and red marks, teachers would send me back to my desk with the order, "MARIAN, READ THE INSTRUCTIONS."

This flaw also affects other areas of my life. My clothing must be washer/dryer friendly, or it goes straight to the dry cleaners. Reading tags taxes my brain. Oh yes, and it's just a given that I will never program any of my electronics because that would require actually reading instructions. And, should I ever have a child, I will need to purchase all toys preassembled, or the poor kid will just have to play with the box. I enlighten you about my quirks so that you will understand the significance of the moment I'm about to describe.

Last summer my friend Jenny and I traveled to North Carolina for a conference. After arriving at the airport and then driving to several convenience stores in search of an Icee machine (I'm a big fan of anything in the Slurpee family), we finally made our way to the conference center in the Smoky Mountains. Two women. Five bags. Three days. A beautiful thing.

So Jenny and I were at the front desk checking into our room when I noticed a stack of bright yellow flyers. Normally I would have ignored them completely, but the four-word heading at the top of the page grabbed my attention: "WARNING! BEWARE OF BEARS."

I was intrigued. Laughing, I showed it to Jenny, who didn't find it funny at all. Now Jenny, she's a girl who actually reads instructions, and she has a slight bear phobia. Who am I kidding? She is petrified of bears. So needless to say, we stopped in the lobby to review the "skills" the conference center thought we needed to know in the event we encountered a bear. (Yeah right . . . as if we would actually see a bear.)

||||||||||||||||||||||||||||||||||||||||||||||||||||||||||||||||||||||||||||||||||||||

WARNING!
BEWARE OF BEARS

Black bears have been seen in this area recently.

Some things to remember if you encounter a bear:

- Do not run. Remain calm, continue facing the bear, and slowly back away.

- Keep children and pets close at hand.

- Make lots of noise. Yell, whistle, and back away . . . slowly.

- Travel in groups.

- Stand upright. Do not kneel or bend over. Wave arms, jackets, or other materials.

- Never approach or corner a bear.

- Be aware of the presence of cubs, and NEVER come between a bear and its cubs.

||||||||||||||||||||||||||||||||||||||||||||||||||||||||||||||||||||||||||||||||||||||

Two hours later . . . .

Unlike our hometown, which is a massive concrete jungle, the Smoky Mountains are lush and beautiful. Needless to say, we were both looking forward to getting outdoors, enjoying nature, and taking in a good view. After unpacking and checking the conference schedule, we decided there was plenty of time before sunset for a hike up to the lookout mountain.

After choosing our route, we hiked straight up a trail that wound along a creek through thick forest. I thought I was in pretty good shape, but my thighs were seriously burning by the time we reached the peak. Once at the top, Jenny and I spent some time talking, praying, and enjoying the view. Realizing the sun was beginning to set, we decided it was time to head back down the mountain.

Ignorance is bliss.

Jenny and I took our time strolling down the trail, having no idea we were walking in bear territory at the worst possible time of day—dusk—which is known in the bear kingdom as feeding time. We were enjoying our ignorance, that is, of course, until we came around a bend and saw a black bear *the size of a Civic* standing right in front of us. No lie. Girls, that bear was ridiculously humongous!

Instantly, we both froze. All I can say is praise God for yellow flyers and short-term memory. Somewhere from our brains' memory storage department flashed the yellow flyer, and we recalled the skills we'd just read.

Whispering to one another, we said . . .

"Stay calm."

"Don't run."

"Wave your arms."

"Make noise."

The bear swiveled its massive neck and stared straight at us. I could see the white of its eyes. It paused oh so briefly—sizing us up—before continuing on into the woods. I so wish it had roared. A good roar would have made the moment perfect.

I was smiling from ear to ear until I looked over at Jenny, who wasn't at all having the same reaction. The color had drained from her face, and she began shaking uncontrollably. No joke . . . she tried to climb a tree. Her expression said it all—sheer terror. She began mumbling something about her

140

"daughters being raised without a mother" and not wanting "to die this way."

I, on the other hand, was so pumped and saying, "We just saw a bear! Can you believe it? We just saw a real-life bear!".

I thought she might hit me. Jenny was not so amused, and being the smarter of the two of us, she reminded me that in order for us to get home we had to continue down the hill, right past the place where the bear was standing. Wake up, blondie! That meant we must go forward into the bear's territory. Remember rule number 6: never approach a bear.

Good thing she reads instructions.

Then I realized this was serious business. I wasn't laughing anymore. The author of *How to Die in the Outdoors* says, "Bear attacks are relatively rare."[10] That being said, he points out that there are exceptions. The author goes on to say:

> When black bears do attack a human, there is no intent of playfulness. The bear is hungry. You are food. They seldom bother even to kill you first. They just grab hold and start munching. You may have the exceedingly unusual opportunity to feel yourself being ripped apart and watch the meal, which is you, in progress. Those wishing not to be black bear food report success from attacking the bear back, beating it on the head and face with anything available, including fists, and otherwise resisting consumption as long as strength allows.[11]

Jenny was right. We were in danger. Realizing this fact, images of me fighting off a bear attack and being chomped as a midnight snack suddenly crossed my mind. I, too, began to panic a little.

Sure, we were frightened, but we did know the skills for survival.

Verbally reviewing our instructions from the yellow flyer, we grabbed big sticks and moved forward "with confidence," yelling and singing loudly. (Bears smell fear.) Our tails were moving so fast down that trail! While we didn't technically run, we did do a fast walk that I'm certain would win some 5k races. Seriously, I didn't know a person could walk that quickly. Obviously we made it back safely, although it did take Jenny's heart about a day to return to a normal rhythm.

We have laughed over and over again about that day. (And other people laugh at us for how much our bear grows in size every time we tell the story.) The one thing we both agree on is the goodness of God and His great timing and protection. We were amazed at how God prepared us by teaching us just a few hours before the encounter the specific skills we needed to know.

I've thought many times, *What if?* What if I didn't know that running was the one thing you are not supposed to do? Our natural reaction in that moment would have been to flee. But that action would have made us bear kibble for sure. Knowing the right skills literally saved our lives.

Here's a fact: You will face a wilderness season.

Each person's faith will be tested. At some point in life you will go through a wilderness. Perhaps you are in one now.

So far I've described for you a few different types of wildernesses and how these specific ones can be overcome.

If facing rejection . . . a girl needs perspective.

If in despair . . . a girl needs hope.

If living with unmet desires . . . a girl needs to rest.

If in the wilderness of temptation . . . a girl must choose to worship.

These are but a few examples. Pain and suffering will strike each one of us in different ways and at different times. Will you come out of yours bitter or better? Will you be a woman who is stronger or weaker in her faith? Will you run to the Lord or run from Him? Will the trial make you or break you?

How we survive our wilderness seasons is a choice. But survival is also a matter of knowing the right skills and applying them. In the following chapters you will learn four skills that are the essentials to *any* wilderness season you will encounter. Study these skills. Put them into memory and into practice, for you never know when you'll turn a corner and find yourself staring straight into the eyes of a black bear the size of a Civic.

From one girlfriend to another, the official wilderness skills for surviving any type of heartbreak are . . .

1. Drink plenty of water!
2. Seek shelter!
3. Beware of snakes!
4. Don't eat the red berries!

chapter 9

Wilderness Skill #1: Drink Plenty of Water

FACT: Water is essential to life.
All life depends upon it and all life contains it.
The average person can survive three weeks without food
but for only three days without water.
IT IS THE NUMBER ONE PRIORITY!
—**JOHN WISEMAN,** *SAS SURVIVAL HANDBOOK*

You are my God. I worship you.
In my heart, I long for you,
as I would long for a stream in a scorching desert.
PSALM 63:1 CEV

Dehydration is not attractive.
I'm just sayin' . . . the bloating, cracked lips, sunken eyes, and dried and shriveled skin don't exactly cause a girl to look her best. A lack of water doesn't alter just the physical appearance. Oh no, dehydration will also flat-out trick a girl's

mind into some serious craziness, causing what is otherwise a sane and stable woman not to be on her best behavior. The desperation for water causes hallucinations and mental confusion, two of the key indicators of extreme dehydration. (I know . . . so far dehydration sounds an awful lot like the breakup flu, doesn't it?)

Although the cause of dehydration is simply a lack of water, the consequences are anything but simple—they are actually catastrophic. Every "how-to" manual, Web site, television survival show, and actual wilderness guide that I have consulted says the same thing: the number one wilderness survival skill is to drink plenty of water. Water is fundamental. Without it, a person could die within thirty-six hours.

Dehydration

Why is water so essential for life? For starters, it comprises roughly three-quarters of the human body: 70 percent of our brains, 82 percent of our blood, 90 percent of our lungs.

On a normal nonwilderness day, your body loses nearly a gallon of water through sweating and urination, and even more if you are hot or exerting a lot of energy. This water must be replaced. Most people need to drink between two and three quarts a day. Yet, when in a stressful situation (i.e., lost in the wilderness), the average person's need increases to four to six quarts a day.

Initially, a dehydrated person develops excessive thirst and becomes irritable, weak, and nauseated. As the condition worsens, a person's mental capacity and coordination will diminish. At this point, it will become difficult for the victim to accomplish even the simplest of tasks. (Girls, does this description sound like anyone you know? Perhaps the person in the mirror?)

Spiritual dehydration proves just as dangerous as physical dehydration. In spiritual dehydration our souls are running on empty and are desperate for something (usually the wrong thing) to quench the thirst. Spiritual dehydration can occur in any type of wilderness (rejection, heartbreak, grief, despair, unmet expectations); therefore, girls, we must be certain to guard against it.

Here are a few warning signs:

- irrational choices (you know, the kind usually made while in meltdown mode)
- grasping at people or things to feel loved or secure
- exhaustion (you know, those days when you don't even want to get out of bed)
- disoriented, confused, and "crazy-place" thinking
- feeling "empty" inside
- snappy
- needy
- plagued by thoughts of fear, doubt, or anxiety
- easily frustrated or irritated (cranky pants)

WILDERNESS ALERT:
IF ANY OF THESE WARNING SIGNS APPLY TO YOU,
DO NOT PUT THIS BOOK DOWN—
YOU MUST KEEP READING!

Soul Thirst

The Bible describes our soul's thirst for God in many colorful and descriptive ways. Psalm 42:1–2 says, "As the deer pants for streams of water, so my soul pants for you, O God. My soul thirsts for God, for the living God" (NIV). This psalm clearly articulates the human condition. Just as God created within each of us a thirst mechanism for water and a hunger mechanism for food, so He also placed within our souls a thirst for Him.

As French philosopher Blaise Pascal once said, "Man was created with a God-shaped vacuum in his soul that can only be filled by God Himself." Essentially, the soul thirst is humanity's need for connection with the Creator.

During His earthly ministry, Jesus gave an invitation to thirsty souls to come to Him and find refreshment. He said, "If anyone thirsts, let him come to Me and drink. He who believes in Me, as the Scripture has said, out of his heart will flow rivers of living water" (John 7:37–38 NKJV).

Girlfriends, the significance of His statement will be oh so clear with a little background scoop. Jesus made this announcement during the celebration of the Feast of Tabernacles. The Jewish people were commanded by the Lord to throw a huge party in memory of how He met their every need during their wilderness journey (from slavery in Egypt into the Promised Land). This feast celebrated the fact that when they were in the desert—desperate, dehydrated, and despairing of life— God provided for them in a supernatural way their primary need . . . water.

Each year the Jewish people descended on Jerusalem for this event. Picture a huge rocking party, kind of like the Super Bowl, except everyone is tailgating at the temple instead of the Superdome. This joyous feast was rich with symbolism. On the last—and the greatest—day of the feast, the high priest would lead the people in a procession from the Temple Mount through the city of Jerusalem to the pool of Siloam. Here, the priest would fill a pitcher with water, and the parade would continue back to the temple. In the midst of thousands of worshippers, the high priest would pour the water from the pitcher onto the altar. I know, I know. Kind of sounds strange to us today, but this act symbolized how the Lord had provided life-giving water for the people and how He would continue to do so each year.

Freeze.

Imagine this scene with me. At the pinnacle of the celebration, with the entire city in complete silence, Jesus arose and cried out for all to hear, "If anyone is thirsty, let him come to Me and drink. . . . 'From his innermost being will flow rivers of living water'" (NASB). That's what I call a scene-stealing moment.

Can you imagine the looks on the people's faces?

Can you imagine the questions?

Jesus made the audacious claim that He is the fulfillment of this Old Testament symbol. He is the Living Water—the source of life for those who walk through any wilderness.

Jesus came to quench our thirst for love, acceptance, peace, and life. He alone can fill our innermost being. And He invites us to come to Him and drink. Here, to "drink" means to believe, to trust, to experience . . . this is far more than simply knowing

148

facts about Jesus. Think about it. Drinking implies experiencing Christ. Forsaking other sources of water—admitting that they will never satisfy—and going to the real thing.

Just this week I heard a Hollywood celebrity say the thing she desires most in life is inner peace. She epitomizes the soul thirst that I've described. Her frenzied and frantic search for fulfillment embodies the desperation, the longing, and the need of the dehydrated. Sadly, this young woman doesn't know Jesus. Her need is the same as yours and mine. The difference is this: if you have a relationship with Jesus Christ, you have access to the Living Water that will quench your thirst. The question is, are you choosing to drink from the real Living Water?

Here's the thing about water: one drink is never enough. When we come in faith to Jesus for salvation, our eternal destiny is secure because of His finished work on the cross. But since we are hardwired for relationship with God, He knows that nothing else and no one else will ever satisfy our thirst. So when Jesus invites us to come and drink, He is extending an invitation to us to find our daily source of life and fulfillment in Him.

The Cure for Dehydration

The smartest thing a girl can do when she finds herself in a wilderness is to drink plenty of water. The inherent challenges and trials require so much strength and energy that her normal reservoir gets tapped out easily, leaving her dehydrated. "Normal" life is difficult enough, but facing a wilderness season without water spells disaster. Consistent, daily, moment-by-moment drinking from the fountain of Living Water—Jesus Christ—cures spiritual dehydration.

I'm sure many of you are asking the obvious question: how do I do this? Relax. I'm the type of girl who would never tell you to do something without telling you how to do it. The following is a great explanation of what it means to drink of Jesus, the Living Water:

> Jesus is not with us in a visible or tangible way. Therefore, he cannot be approached geographically, as he could be when on the earth. Coming to Jesus must be an act of the heart. But what is this movement of the heart? What is this soul-drinking? We say sometimes as we stand before some scene of beauty that we are drinking it in; or changing the metaphor slightly, we say our eyes are feasting on it. What do we mean? We mean that we have put ourselves in a position to behold the beauty . . . . In that way we drink in the scene.

> So it is with Jesus. We first put ourselves in a position to behold him clearly. Since he is not here this is always done through his Word, whether read in the Bible, heard in a sermon, or seen in a life. Jesus said, "The *words* that I have spoken to you are spirit and life" (John 6:63). We meet the life-giving Jesus today in his Word, and when he calls us to come and drink, it is his words to which we come. They carry the living water.[12]

So, how do you drink deeply from God's Word? So glad you asked. Here's a game plan for meeting with Jesus and finding fulfillment and refreshment for your soul.

Drink Deeply from the Living Water

You may call this a "quiet time," or you may refer to it simply as "spending time with Jesus," but however you describe this trip to the Water Fountain, the essentials are the same:

- Set a specific time in your day to meet with Jesus. Find a quiet place and bring your Bible, a journal, and a pen. Depending on the day and the weather, I may meet with Jesus in a park, a coffee shop, or in my home.
- Begin your time with prayer. Ask the Lord to speak to you. Tell God you are thirsty and need refreshing and renewing.
- Choose a book of the Bible and begin reading it from the beginning. As you read, take time to pause and reflect on the words. Don't rush. Absorb the truth.
- Interact with God as you read by asking Him questions. After you ask Him a question, wait for Him to speak. Journal your thoughts and impressions.

Here are a few I ask as I'm reading the Bible:

1. What do I learn about God (the Father, the Son, the Spirit) from this Scripture?
2. What do I learn about myself from this Scripture?
3. What commands/instructions should I obey?
4. What truth can I apply to my life?
5. What sin do I need to confess?
6. What promises can I claim?
7. What does God reveal about my wilderness season?

- If a verse or passage speaks to your situation (i.e., your wilderness season), write the verse down on a note card and carry it with you. Then, as you go to work, school, or just attending to daily life, you can "take a sip" of living water throughout the day.

For example, I wrote Joshua 1:9 on a piece of paper in my car. In that passage God says, "Be strong and courageous! Do not tremble or be dismayed, for the LORD your God is with you wherever you go" (NASB). This Scripture proved a lifeline for me in the darkest days of my wilderness experiences. I would often read that verse and refresh my thirsty heart with those life-giving words. (You will find more "lifeline" Scriptures in the appendix.)

- Conclude this time with prayer. Keeping with the water metaphor, imagine the word *pour* as a guide. When you pray, "pour out" to God your hurt, questions, needs, desires, and petitions. Then ask Jesus to "pour into" you His Spirit. This is called "being filled with the Spirit." (This is when you surrender your will to the Lord through prayer and allow Him to fill you with His love, joy, peace, patience, kindness, goodness, faithfulness, gentleness, and self-control [Gal. 5:22–23 NIV].)

Each day, as you give Jesus control of your life and choose to walk in obedience to His command, He pours His life into you. Through this "filling," Jesus gives us the strength and power for each day. Spending time with Jesus is spiritual hydration.

He alone refuels.

He alone renews.

He alone restores.

He alone refreshes.

Girls, I know it is tempting to turn to relationships, or to shopping, or to the refrigerator, or even to happy hour to fill our emptiness, but those wells are empty and never quench our true thirst. If you neglect time with Jesus, it won't be long until you begin to see those ugly, telltale signs of dehydration creeping into your life.

Hooked on Living Water

One of the biggest blessings from any wilderness experience is the fact that we are reminded of our complete and utter dependence upon God. Just as the body is doomed without water, so we are ruined if we don't turn to Jesus for daily filling. Self-sufficiency is like choosing to walk across a desert without a canteen.

For the woman who chooses to cling to Jesus, it often makes the experience one that she would repeat again because of the deep connection she felt with her God. Just this morning I was walking with my good friend Jennifer. For several years now Jen has longed to be a mother, yet she has endured a wilderness called infertility. As we walked our neighborhood she said to me, "You know, Marian, I'm almost scared to get pregnant now. The past two years have been such a blessing because I've been forced to cling to Jesus. I've found myself desperate to spend time with Him in the Word. I've needed Him to make it through each day. Without the blessing of this wilderness season I would not know Jesus the way I know Him today." She concluded by saying something so powerful: "I don't want to ever get to a point that I think I can make it one minute without Him."

Many of my fellow survivors share with me the same phenomenon. When the heartbreak heals or the emotional storm passes, they find themselves actually missing their wilderness season because of the closeness they experienced with Jesus.

Scientists say the more a person drinks water the more he or she craves it. I know from personal experience that this is true of Jesus. Desperation *for* Him causes a dependency *on* Him that results in a deeper relationship *with* Him. And before you know it, girls, you are hooked. Because nothing, absolutely nothing, can compare with knowing Jesus.

chapter 10

Wilderness Skill #2: Seek Shelter

*Shelter: something beneath, behind, or within
which a person is protected from storms, missiles,
adverse conditions, etc.; a refuge.*
—DICTIONARY.COM

I find myself at a loss for words.

Trust me. This is not the ideal situation for a writer with a deadline. My problem is not a lack of information or writer's block. Actually, quite the opposite is true. I so long to provide women real hope and to teach the skills I've learned that I find myself without the space to say it all. But the main obstacle of the moment is this: how do I even begin to describe to you the most powerful skill I've learned through this experience?

How do I, the simple girl that I am, create sentences to explain the unexplainable? How do I describe something so supernatural that I know my best and most illustrative depiction will always fall short?

As I grapple for the right words to communicate the magnificence of this truth to you, I stop and realize that not until you, the reader, are in a place of desperation where you need this skill—and not until you put into practice what I am about to describe—will this wilderness skill be life changing. But once you appropriate this truth, you will know the unbelievable power found in the name of Jesus.

Shelter

Wilderness experts tell us that, next to the need for water, the most essential requirement for survival in the wild is shelter. A good shelter provides protection from the elements and a sense of safety and security. Concerning our shelter, the Bible says: "The name of the LORD is a strong tower; The righteous runs into it and is safe" (Prov. 18:10 NASB).

Our shelter is the name of the Lord. I know, I know, you are probably asking yourself a very logical question: *how is God's name a shelter?* Throughout the Bible, God's name represents His nature. Whenever the Lord reveals His name, He discloses an aspect of His character.

For instance, when Moses (a guy who led one seriously long wilderness expedition) asked the Lord to demonstrate His glory, God responded by revealing His name *and* His character. Check out how the two are combined in this story:

> Then Moses said, "Please, let me see Your glory."
>
> He [the Lord] said, "I will cause all My goodness to pass in front of you, and I will proclaim the name Yahweh before you. I will be gracious to whom I will

be gracious, and I will have compassion on whom I will have compassion." But He answered, "You cannot see My face, for no one can see Me and live." The LORD said, "Here is a place near Me. You are to stand on the rock, and when My glory passes by, I will put you in the crevice of the rock and cover you with My hand until I have passed by. Then I will take My hand away, and you will see My back, but My face will not be seen." (Exod. 33:18–23)

This is by far one of my all-time favorite moments in Scripture. When I first became a Christian, I read this story and could not get over the fact that Moses saw God's back. I vividly recall sitting in my apartment and reading these words and literally jumping off my bed, saying, "Moses saw God's back! Moses saw God's back!" The image of Moses tucked in a rock and seeing the massive back of the Lord blew me away.

I called my best friend and said, "Did you know that Moses saw God's back?"

She was like, "Yeah, who doesn't know that?"

I was like, "Oh, my gosh!!! This is so unbelievable." (Yes, I know I reveal way too much about my quirky self.)

Back to our story. Moses, a man desperate for hope in the midst of the ultimate wilderness season, begs God for one thing—to see His glory. God's response is so cool that I'm going to shut up now and let the Bible speak for itself:

Moses cut two stone tablets like the first ones. He got up early in the morning, and taking the two stone tablets in his hand, he climbed Mount Sinai, just as the LORD had commanded him.

The LORD came down in a cloud, stood with him there, and proclaimed [His] name Yahweh. Then the LORD passed in front of him and proclaimed:

Yahweh—Yahweh is a compassionate and gracious God, slow to anger and rich in faithful love and truth, maintaining faithful love to a thousand [generations], forgiving wrongdoing, rebellion, and sin. But He will not leave [the guilty] unpunished, bringing the consequences of the fathers' wrongdoing on the children and grandchildren to the third and fourth generation. (Exod. 34:4–7)

There, in the cleft of the rock, Moses is given a glimpse of God's glory. In this revelation, God discloses His name and His nature: He is Yahweh, the self-existent One. He is good. He is faithful. He is compassionate and just. He is slow to anger and abounding in love.

Who wouldn't run in a full sprint to this God? If, in your wilderness, you hesitate to run to Him, you might want to revisit who you think God is. If your image of God doesn't line up with His revelation of who He is, then you very well are believing some lies of the Enemy about God's character. My God, the God revealed in the Bible, is One a girl can run to when life gets scary.

Speaking of running, that is exactly what we do in the wilderness. We bolt because we are afraid.

We fear the unknown.

We fear the future.

We fear being rejected . . . again.

We fear being hurt, exposed, humiliated, or overlooked.

We fear that the Enemy is right, that this world is without hope.

We fear that our circumstances are too big for God to handle.

Girls, fear sends us into meltdown mode, and when our emotions go to the "crazy place," we dash about searching for shelter (security and protection) wherever we think we can find it. The wilderness reveals our hearts. We either run to the Lord or away from Him. The decision is our own. But as we've seen, there is only one truly safe shelter, and that is the name of the Lord.

Strength in Weakness

I'll be flat-out honest. I learned this skill from desperation. Over and over again during my wilderness season, I battled a fierce onslaught of fear. The kind that is physical—you know, when your stomach is in knots and your chest tightens. I think they call this being "gripped" by fear. However you choose to describe it, fear isn't fun.

I was fighting rejection at every turn, and my mind was constantly tormented by the "what ifs" and the unknowns of the future (the wilderness of unmet desires). In addition, I had the added joy of the Enemy assaulting my faith (the wilderness of temptation). So when I wasn't in the pit of despair, fear tried to control me.

It was brutal.

One night when I was at my absolute weakest and I didn't have the strength to fight the Enemy's lies with God's truth, all

I could muster was the ability to say out loud, "Jesus." Through brokenness and tears, I simply cried out, "Jesus." Ironically, at my point of ultimate weakness, I found my greatest strength.

As I cried out, "Jesus," I felt His peace descend and knew I was surrounded by His presence. In that moment I had this overwhelming comfort that He was shielding me from my Enemy. In desperation I ran to the name of the Lord, and He became my shelter, my refuge . . . my hiding place. When I spoke His name, He covered me.

I can't explain to you how and why this works. I just know that it does. (Much like electricity, while I can't explain the physics, I sure know the power.) The name of Jesus is so powerful because God the Father made His name supreme:

> For this reason [Christ's suffering and death on the
>   cross] God also highly exalted Him
> and gave Him the name that is above every name,
> so that at the name of Jesus every knee should bow—
> of those who are in heaven and on earth and
>   under the earth—
> and every tongue should confess that Jesus Christ
>   is Lord,
> to the glory of God the Father. (Phil. 2:9–11)

The one thing I am certain of is this: there is no name higher or greater than the name of Jesus.

His name speaks of His power and authority.

His name silences the Enemy.

His name is supernatural.

His name is above all names.

As the old hymn says, "There's just something about that name!"

Meltdown

When I think about this wilderness skill, I can't help but remember a conversation I had with a friend of mine. Borrowing my favorite phrase, she called and said, "Marian, please come over! I am having a meltdown." What was the crisis? She was going through a horrific breakup, and the thought of the looming separation and potential years of singleness began to overwhelm her. She was staring fear straight in the eyes. While her situation may be different than your own, put yourself in her shoes and imagine the issue in your life that sends you into a full-throttle, emotional freak-out.

Arriving at her house a little while later, I took one look at her and knew she was in the "crazy place." Her emotions were erratic, and she was weeping like a woman who had no hope that her life would be OK. I listened to her sob for a while until I couldn't take it anymore, and the truth-speaker in me said, "Girl, we've got to pull it together and focus on who your God is!"

Fear crept in because her focus shifted from the person and promises of God to the "what ifs" and the "unknowns" of the future. Sitting at her kitchen table, which was now littered with meltdown evidence (tissues, junk food, and Diet Coke), we began to pray.

For starters, we simply said the name of "Jesus" over and over again. "Jesus, You are the Prince of Peace, Mighty God, King of Kings, Lord of Lords . . . Jesus." Together she and I called on His name. We said His name until she could remember there is One greater than any storm she will face, One who has walked through the wilderness on her behalf, and One who is right now fighting for her. After a few minutes of simply saying the name of Jesus, her hysterical crying turned to peaceful breathing. She was now safe in the shelter of His name.

Then I said, "You need to begin praising God out loud, right now, for who He is and for what He has done, for fear is banished with faith." Softly she began to whisper praise to God for His righteousness, holiness, goodness, and power. After a few minutes her voice was stronger, and she praised Him for His wisdom, His love, His sovereignty, and His grace. Now I could see her faith was beginning to take over, and she began to say aloud the power and purpose of God in her situation. After a few minutes we stopped praying and looked at each other and knew she was clear of the crazy place—for she made the choice to run to the shelter of the name of the Lord.

chapter 11

Wilderness Skill #3: Beware of Snakes

FACT:
To catch or kill a snake, first stun it with a thrown rock or stick,
and then use the forked end of a long stick to pin its head
to the ground. Kill it with a rock, knife, or another stick.
Be careful throughout this procedure,
especially when dealing with poisonous snakes.
[I personally love this next nugget.]
Snakes can be cooked in any fashion,
but all should be skinned and gutted.
[two words: yeah, right]

GREGORY J. DAVENPORT, *WILDERNESS SURVIVAL* (2ND ED.)

Few of us will ever forget the first time we watched the film *The Passion of the Christ.* The sheer magnitude of Christ's sufferings left most viewers speechless and many breathless. In this film the familiar words of Scripture come crashing through our senses in living color. The prophetic words "by His stripes we are healed" (Isa. 53:5 NKJV) take on a whole new meaning when watching the brutal scourging of Jesus.

I recall sitting in the theater and begging "Jesus" not to get up when He had fallen at the whipping post. "Don't stand up!" I repeated over and over again under my breath as I watched the Roman soldiers rip the skin from His back. "Please, don't stand up." I thought if I could encourage Him to stay down then His suffering would end. Yet, He didn't stay down. No, He stood and took more lashes and more lashes—for He knew that His brokenness would mean our wholeness. His death would mean our life.

It stunned me how relieved I was when the crucifixion finally arrived, for with death my Savior's suffering would finally end. Whoever thought death would be a welcomed sight? I'm pretty sure I held my breath for most of the movie.

Amazing sacrifice.

Amazing love.

Amazing grace.

As difficult as this movie was for me to watch, one scene in particular caused my heart to stand up and cheer. I absolutely loved the very first scene. The movie begins with a heavily burdened Jesus praying in the Garden of Gethsemane. There, in the garden, just hours before His arrest, Christ surrenders Himself to the will of God the Father. From the following scene of *The Passion of the Christ,* we, the audience, are given a glimpse of the future victory and triumph that will come through His death.

But first there is a conversation:

"Do you really believe that one man can bear the full burden of sin?" taunts the voice of Satan.

Jesus, with his eyes heavenward and speaking only to the Father says, "I trust in you."

And then, continuing his accusations, Satan says, "Saving their souls is too costly."

And Jesus says to the Father, "Not my will, but yours be done."[13]

What is this dialogue? Has Mel Gibson taken creative license? No. I think this scene perfectly encapsulates the entire cosmic drama of the Crucifixion: God became man in order to redeem humanity from our slavery to sin and Satan. In doing so, Jesus must face the same temptations you and I face. So while Jesus agonizes about His impending death, Satan tempts Him to abandon His mission to redeem the world's sins.

Let us never forget that Jesus is God in the flesh—fully God *and* fully man. So, there in the garden, it is Jesus the *man* who must make the choice to endure the pain and suffering for our sin. At Gethsemane, Jesus determines He will go forward with God's plan and redeem humanity. He will be the perfect substitute, and He will lay down His life to die in our place. But His surrender doesn't come easily.

Can you fathom how tempting it must have been for Him to think only of Himself?

Meanwhile, another presence lurks in the garden that night—a snake. While Jesus is praying, a serpent, symbolizing Satan, slithers toward the Son of God to make a deadly strike. But then, at the last second, with eyes fixed, Jesus rises to His feet and with one step crushes the head of the serpent—a step that defines His destiny. A historical moment. A prophetic moment. A moment that symbolizes the victory that is soon to come. He will crush the head of the serpent. Satan will be defeated.

Girls, let me just take a commercial interlude right here and fill you in on a little fact about yours truly: I hate snakes.

Let me explain. I loathe snakes. Rats, I'm not a fan of either—given the whole plague thing and all—but I can handle them. Spiders, bring 'em on. But snakes, there is nothing I hate more than a snake. So when Jesus stood to His feet and stomped the serpent's head, I was elated.

But my elation had more to do with the fact that this serpent represents Satan. The Deceiver, the Accuser, the one whom Jesus calls the Father of Lies, the one who is the cause of all anguish and suffering in this world. And since the beginning of time (back in a different garden called Eden), the serpent has become synonymous with Satan himself.

But girls, *Gethsemane is not the first time Jesus has faced the serpent.*

When Jesus began His earthly ministry, He, too, went into the wilderness. There He was tested and tempted by Satan. In Jesus's wilderness season we learn an extremely important wilderness skill: Jesus shows us *how* to stand against the lies and deceptions of the Enemy.

> Then Jesus was led up by the Spirit into the wilderness to be tempted by the Devil. After He had fasted 40 days and 40 nights, He was hungry. Then the tempter approached Him and said, "If You are the Son of God, tell these stones to become bread."
>
> But He answered, "*It is written:* Man must not live on bread alone but on every word that comes from the mouth of God."
>
> Then the Devil took Him to the holy city, had Him stand on the pinnacle of the temple, and said to Him, "If You are the Son of God, throw Yourself down. For it is written: He will give His angels orders concerning

you, and they will support you with their hands so that you will not strike your foot against a stone."

Jesus told him, "*It is also written:* Do not test the Lord your God."

Again, the Devil took Him to a very high mountain and showed Him all the kingdoms of the world and their splendor. And he said to Him, "I will give You all these things if You will fall down and worship me."

Then Jesus told him, "Go away, Satan! *For it is written:* Worship the Lord your God, and serve only Him."

Then the Devil left Him, and immediately angels came and began to serve Him. (Matt. 4:1–11)

When Christ was tempted by Satan in the wilderness, each temptation came back to one thing: doubt. If you will notice, every time Satan speaks he begins his question with the word *if*.

- If you are the Son of God, then . . . (Satan wants Jesus to doubt His identity as the Son of God.)
- If you will worship me . . . (Satan wants Jesus to doubt His redemptive mission and take a shortcut around the cross.)

Satan's ploy was to use questions to tempt Jesus into sin (i.e., not trusting God the Father.) Doesn't that ole snake do the same thing with you and me?

- If God really loved you, then . . . (The snake wants you to doubt God's heart for you.)
- If God is really good, then He wouldn't allow . . . (The snake wants you to doubt the character of God.)
- If you were really a Christian, then . . . (The snake would love it if you would doubt your own salvation.)

Beware! Just as a snake disguises itself in tall brush and rocks, Satan deceives you and me with questions and accusations while in the wilderness. He is oh so subtle.

But in this interchange between Christ and Satan, we see a snapshot of how we should respond when encountering the snake in the wilderness. Each time Jesus replied to Satan's suggestive questions with three simple words: "It is written." And then, Jesus spoke out loud a truth from Scripture in response to the lies of the Enemy. Finally, Jesus took authority over Satan and commanded him to leave.

Isn't this is an amazing wilderness skill? And it may very well be the best-kept secret in all of Christianity. As believers in Jesus Christ, you and I can do the very same thing today. But where do we begin? We must start by taking inventory of our thoughts and making certain we aren't listening to or believing the lies of the Enemy. But how does a girl know if she is being fed a lie? I'm so glad you asked.

True story: At times in my life, I've been what you would call a slave to fashion. Shopping can be a problem for me. Some girls emotionally eat . . . I emotionally spend. Jesus and I are working on this.

So a few years ago I had a major fashion crush on this new pair of jeans. Problem A: my budget could not afford this specific pair of designer denim. Problem B: my budget could not afford this specific pair of designer denim. But girls, let me just say . . . I so loved these jeans. I would go visit them at the department store and just stare at them. Sometimes I would try them on and ponder whether I really needed to pay rent that month. Images of my homeless self in designer denim would send me out the door empty-handed.

Then a friend of mine kindly informed me that I could probably buy the jeans on the Internet at a much better price. Brilliant! I'm so in for a bargain. So now, empowered with shopping scoop, I surfed droves of denim on eBay until I discovered a pair that was identical to the ones I'd been eyeing in the store. And do you want to know the best part? They were brand new and cost only a fraction of the price.

I bought those bad boys faster than Nicole Ritchie changes sunglasses. But I did uncover one major bummer to online shopping. There is no instant-gratification-wear-the-jeans-tonight thrill. So, I waited (and if you will recall, I love to wait) a few days for the UPS guy to deliver my new duds. Giddy, I ripped open the package only to discover that I'd been fashion punked.

They were soooooooooooooo counterfeit!

I'm sure you are dying to know how I knew the jeans were as fake as a tan in January. It's simple, really. I knew the moment I touched the fabric that these babies were not the real thing. You wanna know how? Because I'd seen, touched, and tried on the "real thing" enough times to know a fraud a mile away.

Here's my point, ladies: to spot a lie, you must know the truth.

Remember . . .

Satan wants to deceive you about who you are.

Satan wants to deceive you about God's character.

Satan wants to deceive you about God's plan and purpose for your life.

And when in a wilderness season (i.e., hurting, lonely, sad, depressed), you and I make one easy target for his lies. Please note: this snake is sneaky. Satan watched and waited, and only when Jesus became hungry for food did the Enemy unleash his taunts and temptations.

Hunger is defined as "a strong or compelling desire or craving." Satan waited until Jesus was physically hungry for food, and then it was that specific desire that the Enemy zeroed in on when tempting Jesus not to trust His heavenly Father.

A woman in a wilderness can "hunger" for so many things that make her prime for temptation, such as love, affection, attention, affirmation, relief from stress, or even an escape from pain. I tell you this as a warning: carefully consider what you are thinking about. If you are going through a tough time and find yourself experiencing tormenting thoughts or strong temptations, you very well may be dealing with a snake in the grass.

My friend Amy told me about the wilderness season she walked through following her painful divorce. When she married right after college, she expected it would be forever—aka 'til death do us part. Yet weeks into the marriage, her fairy tale became a nightmare as her "Prince Charming" husband became both physically and verbally abusive.

Even with biblical grounds for divorce, Amy candidly admits that Satan took full advantage of her pain and her hunger for love to heap lies and accusations on her. Here are a few lies Amy heard in her wilderness:

- God will never forgive you.
- You are used goods now. You might as well give yourself away to any guy who comes along.
- A "real" Christian man would never marry a girl like you.
- Why don't you numb your pain with alcohol and male attention?

It took time for Amy to learn to silence Satan with the Word of God and to take her rightful authority as a redeemed girl and tell him to "be gone." Through Bible study and involvement with other Christian women, she has learned this skill. Today she is a wonderful example to many that Satan is a big, fat liar. Amy not only actively serves in her church discipling young women but is also married to one of the godliest men I know. Amy's testimony is one of victory because she made the decision to stop believing Satan's lies and to start standing in God's truth.

This wilderness skill is so huge! Our thoughts must be based upon truth, or we will be in big trouble. The reason? Our thoughts lead to our emotions, and our emotions lead to our actions. And when we are in the wilderness (i.e., rejection, loss, despair), it doesn't take much to send a girl's emotional state of being into full-blown meltdown. We have to be so careful to not entertain the lies of the Enemy and allow him to dictate our emotions and our actions. Determine, especially in wilderness seasons, to stand in truth.

I know someone reading this may be thinking, *Hold it right there, missy. What, exactly, is truth?* Girls, there is a definitive answer to this infamous question. The word *truth* means "that which has fidelity (conformity) to the original." Meaning? There is a standard. Given that the word itself implies there is a measurement of what is "true," then it only makes sense that truth is not relative.

Then what is truth? God's Word is truth. Jesus said in His prayer for you and me before His death on the cross, "Sanctify them [purify, consecrate, separate them for Yourself, make them holy] by the Truth; Your Word is Truth" (John 17:17 AMP).

Jesus teaches us that the Bible, God's very Word, is the truth. So what's my point? If my thoughts about myself or about my God differ with what God has spoken, then I am believing a lie. Remember my denim debacle? I recognized a fraud only because I knew the real thing.

Jesus also gives us a warning about the snake, Satan, when He cautions, "The thief comes only to steal and kill and destroy; I have come that they may have life, and have it to the full" (John 10:10 NIV). Satan has an agenda, and his mode of operation has not changed; he operates in lies. But girls, listen carefully—the snake is defeated! Jesus defanged the serpent at the cross. All he can do is lie to us. We must choose whether we will listen to his lies or to God's truth.

Looking back over my recent wilderness season, I recognize that so many of my issues came down to where I allowed my thoughts to dwell. The Enemy desired not only to steal my worship but also to kill my joy and destroy my faith. I've found the same to be true for every woman I've interviewed in writing this book. Countless women shared their wilderness tales with me, and the common denominator in all of them was the torment of lies and accusations each woman endured.

So, what's a girl to do? We must do what Christ modeled for us in the wilderness. Resist Satan and stand firm in the truth of God's Word. Just as it says in James 4:7, "Submit yourselves, then, to God. Resist the devil, and he will flee from you" (NIV).

Submit—turn to God in prayer and claim His truth. I suggest you find specific Scripture passages that deal with the particular lies (temptations, questions, accusations) that torment you.

Resist—say no to the lies and tell Satan to "go away in the name of Jesus."

No lie. Just last night I put this skill into practice. I was driving to a dinner party when I felt those "poor me" thoughts forming. I listened to a few and realized if I didn't nip them in the bud, I would be quite the dud at dinner. So I began responding to the negative thoughts (lies) with God's Word. For each lie I heard, I spoke a Scripture out loud. Finally, as I was pulling up to the valet I said, "Satan, go away in the name of Jesus." And guess what? It turns out that Jesus proves one excellent wilderness guide. Though the snake was indeed dead, I opted for something else for dinner. No "skinning and gutting" for this girl.

chapter 12

Wilderness Skill #4: Don't Eat the Red Berries

FACT:
Belladonna is a beautiful plant that grows wild
in the United States. By the way, its berries, though they look
edible, are deadly. Initially the poison causes dry mouth and
difficulty swallowing. And then, the following symptoms occur:
skin will grow warm, heartbeat quickens, and then the pupils will
dilate. Eating this poisonous berry causes blood pressure
to rise and the heartbeat to become erratic. The mind will
wander into delirium and confusion. Eventually the respiratory
drive will progressively fail . . . causing death.
[Note to self: carry a protein bar into the woods to curb hunger.]
BUCK TILTON, *HOW TO DIE IN THE OUTDOORS*

It was so surreal watching my husband load the U-Haul with everything he wanted to take with him: his clothes, his books, his pictures—everything that is, of course, except me,

174

his wife." Becky is a godly woman in every sense of the word. Her deep love for the Lord and depth of relationship with Jesus has much to do with the fact that Becky has survived a wilderness season that was wrought with pain, injustice, rejection, and disappointment. Her testimony is one that inspires and challenges many Christians. Her story reveals brokenness and obedience, death and life:

I stood in our driveway with tears flowing down my cheeks, in utter disbelief that our marriage was really over. Yet, he was leaving. He didn't want to be married anymore. What does that even mean? I couldn't process all that was happening.

I remember walking with him to the truck and positioning myself by the driver's side door. He was forced to step around me—without looking me in the eye—in order to get inside his escape vehicle. I told him, "I love you, and I want our marriage to work."

He was silent. Not a word. I didn't get one single word from him . . . the man I had known and loved for so many years.

Standing cemented to the spot where I had just begged for my marriage, I watched as my husband drove away and stared motionless into the distance until he turned out of sight.

Devastation.

In an instant my whole world turned upside down. So many emotions flooded my way: an onslaught of rejection, fear, despair, and unbelievable grief. Turning toward what was once "our" house, I walked inside and threw myself onto the sofa.

In a prayer-like plea I asked the Lord, "What am I going to do now?" Jesus answered my question with a question of His own. The Lord said to me, "Becky, there are two paths before you. One is a path that many people choose; it is a road called bitterness. This way is easy and well traveled. The other path, while much more difficult, is the path of love. The first path leads to death, for it is a poison that will slowly kill you. The second, My Way, leads to life. Becky, which do you choose?"

This was not the response I expected from the Lord, but I know without question that it was He who spoke to me that day. A choice lay before me: choose life or choose death. Choose to indulge bitterness or choose a different way—to love, to forgive, to bless. There wasn't really an option, was there? I knew, as I know at this moment, I had to choose the way of life.

There is a way that seems right to a man,
but its end is the way to death. (Prov. 14:12)

Beware of Bitterness

In a wilderness season, women who are hurting, alone, afraid, and hungry for relief face a huge temptation to feed their souls with something that will actually harm them—the "red berry" called bitterness. Jesus warned my friend Becky that bitterness leads to death. Yet many people choose this way. What do I mean when I say they "choose" bitterness? Whenever a person lives feeling entitled to her anger and justified in her resentment, she chooses to allow a bitter poison to brew in her heart. This poison slowly destroys her from the inside out.

The Bible warns us about bitterness: "See to it that no one comes short of the grace of God; that no root of bitterness springing up causes trouble, and by it many be defiled" (Heb. 12:15 NASB). God tells us in Scripture that a root of bitterness causes trouble and defiles many. Imagine that a person's life is like a fruit tree. A tree contains a root system that digs into the ground. Roots provide life and nourishment for the tree. Fruit grows simply as the outward manifestation of the root. Now, if the root of a tree is bitter, what will the fruit of that tree taste like?

I know a girl who has not heeded this warning. Bitterness absolutely controls her. Her life is like a cup filled with a poisonous liquid. If people get close enough to bump into her "cup," the poison spills out and harms those around her. What happened to this girl? Like my friend Becky, she experienced some horrific circumstances in her past: abuse, abandonment, and rejection. But, unlike Becky, she chose the other path of anger, hatred, resentment, and unforgiveness. At this point, she has not dealt with the root of bitterness in her soul, and the poison is literally destroying her body, mind, soul, and spirit . . . not to mention her relationships.

I've discovered from examining my own life and from ministering to other women that bitterness occurs in a woman's heart from three primary sources: unhealed wounds, unmet expectations, and unforgiveness. For our wilderness skills we must learn how to deal with each of these so that bitterness doesn't consume and destroy our lives.

Unhealed Wounds

There is something interesting in the definition of bitterness:

bit·ter \ bit-er \ *adjective*

- having a harsh, disagreeably acrid taste
- causing pain; piercing; stinging: *a bitter chill*
- Characterized by intense antagonism or hostility: *bitter hatred*
- hard to admit or accept: *a bitter lesson.* resentful or cynical: *bitter words*

[Origin: bef. 1000; ME, OE *biter;* c. G *bitter,* ON *bitr,* Goth *baitrs;* akin to BITE][14]

Notice that the origin of the word *bitter* is "bite." If you've ever been bitten—be that by a dog, a spider, or a four-year-old—you know that a bite inflicts pain. A wound results, and if it is not taken care of, it can become infected—poisonous to the body. Likewise, if we don't take care of our emotional "wounds," our souls become infected with poison.

Are you in a wilderness season as a result of a painful event? a breakup? a divorce? a rejection? an accusation? or just plain disappointment? If so, there is a wound inside of you that you must deal with or it will turn to bitterness.

And I have great news! Jesus is your Great Physician, and He longs to heal your hurts and bandage your wounds. Isaiah 61:1, a prophetic passage about Christ, describes His life and ministry by saying that He will "bind up the brokenhearted" (NIV). The word *bind* in the original language literally means "to bandage, to cover, to enclose, to envelope." I love this picture. In it, I see Christ taking the broken pieces of our lives and

178

binding them together with His love and making them whole. But we must choose to go to Jesus with our hurting hearts so that the wound does not become infected.

It would take more paper than Office Depot has in stock to write of my wounds that Christ has healed. When I first came into relationship with Jesus, I was a girl overflowing with bitterness. Honestly, I just thought it was normal to be angry, easily offended, untrusting, and critical of other people's faults. I had no idea these attitudes and actions were the fruit of bitterness in my heart. But soon after I surrendered my life to Christ, He started putting His Great Physician finger into some of my old wounds and asking, "Does it hurt when I poke here?"

"Yeeeeeeeeeeeeeees, that hurts!" I would scream, wanting to jump off the examining table. But Jesus continued to press. God revealed my unhealed wounds by allowing circumstances in my life to expose unresolved issues of rejection, abandonment, and shame. He used Scripture to speak truth to me about my sin that was rooted in bitterness, and He used godly friends to speak words of life to me. Dealing with unhealed wounds can be painful—and, frankly, still isn't fun—but the process brings wholeness.

Knowing this to be true, I realized when I walked through my most recent wilderness experience that I needed to let Jesus heal my hurt immediately before it became infected and caused more problems down the road (e.g., becoming bitter and jaded to the point that I couldn't trust someone in my next relationship).

Girls, it is absolutely crucial that we deal with our spiritual wounds. Don't stuff the emotions down and pretend you're "fine." If pain goes unaddressed, it causes bitterness. So here's what I want you to do. Repeat after me these three statements:

1. I WILL NOT STUFF MY EMOTIONS. (Allow yourself time to grieve. The "wound" could have happened ten days ago or ten years ago. Either way, you need to let yourself deal with it. We get stuck emotionally when we choose to stuff instead of to heal.)

2. I WILL GET REAL BEFORE GOD. (Do what my friends and I like to call "vomit prayers." It's quite an unpleasant description, I know, but they are effective. Get real before God and lay your wounded heart before Him. Tell God where it hurts and ask Him to bind up your wound.)

3. I WILL ASK FOR HELP. (Some wounds need special care. It is important to realize that sometimes we need help processing our pain and grief. Go to a trusted leader at your church and ask him or her to direct you to someone who can help with your specific situation.)

Unmet Expectations

I've often heard it said that the difference between expectations and reality is pain. Think about that for a minute. The higher the level of expectation and the lower the level of reality equals the difference, which is the degree of pain a person experiences. And as we know, pain (left unattended) results in bitterness. Take the prime-time expectation day of the year for example—Valentine's Day. Girls, be honest; expectations are the killer on this day, aren't they? Imagine a girl who all day long is expecting flowers, a candlelit dinner, romantic words, and, of course, jewelry. In her mind these things are what will make her feel loved and important. Then, when reality hits and she finds herself empty-handed, you know the girl is feeling disappointed, and what's the word I'm searching for . . . oh yes, *bitter.*

EXPECTATIONS - REALITY = PAIN

I'll be really honest. When life didn't go according to Plan Marian, I was tempted to eat the red berries. My expectations and my reality did not match up at all. The difference between what I allowed myself to believe and the actual outcome of events was huge. Therefore, my level of pain and disappointment was proportional. Hear me out. I'm not saying expectations are wrong. What I am saying is that we must be extremely careful of what expectations we build in our minds and, ultimately, of where we are placing our hope. If I've learned one thing from this whole ordeal, it is this (and girls, this one is for free): unmet expectations that cause bitterness are often the result of a misplaced hope.

The Lord is teaching me to be extremely careful where I place my hope. Most of us are unaware of how often we place our hope in what we expect to happen or how we expect someone to respond or act. Doing so always leads to disappointment. And disappointment can lead to anger, resentment, and, you guessed it, bitterness.

The biggest unmet expectation is when we place the burden of our happiness or completion upon someone or something other than God. If I expect a friendship or relationship will "make me feel loved or secure," then I will be disappointed with my friend when he or she fails to meet my needs. If I expect marriage or a career to make me feel significant or important, then I will be extremely frustrated when they don't do the job.

Ask yourself this question, "What unmet expectations are causing bitterness in my heart?"

The Bible teaches us the solution to our expectation problem. Check out the following verses and notice where hope is placed in each:

> I wait for the LORD; I wait,
> and put my _hope in His word_.
> I [wait] for the LORD
> more than watchmen for the morning—
> more than watchmen for the morning.
> Israel, put your _hope in the LORD_.
> For there is faithful love with the LORD,
> and with Him is redemption in abundance.
>
> (Ps. 130:5–7, emphasis mine)
>
> but those who _hope in the LORD_
> will renew their strength.
> They will soar on wings like eagles;
> they will run and not grow weary,
> they will walk and not be faint.
>
> (Isa. 40:31 NIV, emphasis mine)

[handwritten note: not my own intellect = my grades]

Where is hope to be put according to these verses? It is to be put _in the Lord_. When I was a little girl, my grandmother had something she called a hope chest. In that old wooden box she placed her treasures. I remember lifting the heavy lid and peering into the box at its contents. Inside I discovered jewelry, family photographs, corsages—things that she wanted to keep "safe." A hope chest helps me to understand what is meant by hope in the Lord. Our expectations, dreams, desires, and hopes have only one safe place, and that is in Him.

Looking back over my recent wilderness season, I now understand why the Lord also caused a "dating desert" during the months following my breakup. He knew during that painful time I would be tempted to turn to another guy instead of to Jesus and to place my hopes in a new relationship instead of in Christ. This was a hard lesson to learn. As I said, my pride didn't like it one bit. But now, I know it was for my good. God knew if my hope was in anything other than Him, then I would ultimately be disappointed. And as we know, a buildup of disappointment turns to bitterness.

- Has your wilderness experience left you with some unmet expectations?
- Can you look back and see that your hope was in something or someone other than Christ?
- Is that disappointment causing pain?

If so, go to the Lord in prayer and ask for His help so that bitterness does not grow in your heart. The following prayer is only a suggestion. Make it your own, but I advise you to include two key elements: surrender and confession.

Father, forgive me for placing my hope in anything (a person, a parent, a promotion, a plan) but You. I know the unmet expectation has caused bitterness in my heart. Forgive me for feeling entitled to my plan. Forgive me for being angry that I did not get my way. You know what is best. I surrender my life to You—*have Your way in me. I choose to let You be God.*

I confess that You alone are the only safe place for my hope. *Help me to guard my thoughts from hoping in something or someone that will not and cannot meet my needs. Please remove the bitterness of unmet expectation from my heart.*

I ask this in the name of Christ Jesus. Amen.

Unforgiveness

Have you ever heard Debbie Ford's expression "Unforgiveness is the poison you drink every day hoping that the other person will die"? That statement is a little harsh, I know, but it is so very true. Unforgiveness is the number one cause of bitterness. Refusing to forgive will flat-out destroy a person. Perhaps this is why Jesus repeatedly commanded us to forgive—He knew it was for our own good.

Take note of the importance of forgiveness when Jesus instructed the disciples how to pray:

Therefore, you should pray like this:

Our Father in heaven, Your name be honored as holy.

Your kingdom come. Your will be done on earth as it is in heaven.

Give us today our daily bread.

And forgive us our debts, as we also have forgiven our debtors.

And do not bring us into temptation, but deliver us from the evil one.

[For Yours is the kingdom and the power and the glory forever. Amen.]

For if you forgive people their wrongdoing, your heavenly Father will forgive you as well. But if you don't forgive people, your Father will not forgive your wrongdoing. (Matt. 6:9–15)

Jesus was asked by the disciples about forgiveness: "Then Peter came to Jesus and asked, 'Lord, how many times shall I forgive my brother when he sins against me? Up to seven times?' Jesus answered, 'I tell you, not seven times, but seventy-seven times'" (Matt. 18:21–22 NIV).

What does it mean to forgive? To answer this question I first want to explain what it doesn't mean. First, forgiveness doesn't mean that we call something that's wrong "right." Forgiveness also isn't excusing behavior or denying that something bad has happened. And here's the thing that trips most people up: forgiveness is not dependent on whether or not the person asks for forgiveness.

So, what is forgiveness? It is simply releasing a debt that you feel is owed. The word *release* is huge. For if we do not choose to let go, we are bound to the person that we feel has wronged us. Is there bitterness in your heart today because of unforgiveness? If you answer yes to any of these questions, there may be someone you need to forgive.

- Do you struggle with anger toward the one who hurt you?
- Do you imagine ways of getting even or getting revenge?
- Do you still rehearse "speeches" that you'd like to deliver?

A Call to the Cross

A Call to the Cross was the title of messages my friends Jason and Susannah Baker spoke to a group of high school students the week before Easter. The series was based on the subject you would expect—the death and resurrection of Jesus Christ. Their primary focus this particular Passion Week was the question: what does it mean to be men and women of the cross?

Their teaching was powerful. The last message, Thursday morning, was different in nature—for that morning we came together to focus on prayer. At the front of the room was stationed a large wooden cross—the emblem of our faith. During that prayer time my friend Susannah spoke of forgiveness. She called this group of teenagers to come to the cross and do in a physical sense what the cross represents—forgive. Forgiveness means to release a debt that you feel someone owes you. To let go and release the one who has offended you.

A simple act was required: write the name of the person you need to forgive on a card and lay it down at the foot of the cross.

In the crowd of high school students was one broken and convicted teacher. Until that moment she did not know that she was holding on to unforgiveness. But as the message of the cross—forgive because you, too, have been forgiven—was spoken, she knew in her heart that God was calling her to lay it down. She was beginning to recognize red berries of bitterness, and in her heart she felt "owed" an apology . . . or at the very least an explanation.

Friends, I was that woman. With a strong nudge from the Holy Spirit, I stood from my seat, walked toward the cross, and placed a small note card on the floor beneath its rugged beams. On it was the name of the one whom I felt owed me a debt. As I kneeled before the cross I let go. I surrendered my right to be "right." I released the one I felt owed me, and I asked forgiveness for my own pride and lack of obedience.

Girls, this is the way of the cross. We meet the person or persons who we think have hurt us or who have offended us at the foot of the cross and forgive because we have been forgiven. In the book of Colossians, notice what Christians are commanded to do in response to the cross: "Therefore, as God's chosen people, holy and dearly loved, clothe yourselves with compassion, kindness, humility, gentleness and patience. Bear with each other and forgive whatever grievances you may have against one another. Forgive as the Lord forgave you. And over all these virtues put on love, which binds them all together in perfect unity. Let the peace of Christ rule in your hearts, since as members of one body you were called to peace. And be thankful" (3:12–15 NIV).

In case you don't know this yet, let me just tell you that God has a huge sense of humor and He is an amazing Teacher— One that likes to give pop quizzes. The following morning, Good Friday, I went to work as usual. At that time I was teaching Bible to juniors at a private Christian school. Since it was Good Friday and the message of the cross was oh so fresh and relevant, I thought my students should read through the entire crucifixion story in our class time. We chose the Gospel of Matthew and read the Passion story, beginning with Jesus's arrest all the way until His glorious resurrection.

I didn't just do this exercise once. No, as the teacher, I read this story out loud five times in the course of the morning. Word by word, stripe by stripe, nail by nail. By the end of the day my heart overflowed with awe for God's glory and a fresh love for Jesus for the price He paid for my sin.

Quiz time.

As I left school that day, I walked to the parking lot and ran straight into none other than my ex-boyfriend. It was like God said, "Please, get out a number two pencil and a piece of paper." At that moment the decision I made at the cross just a day before was put to the test.

When I saw him, I knew I had a choice. I could duck and hide—as I had done many times before—or I could walk toward him. I chose the latter. And girls, with that step came a flood of something that was not of me—it was a river of life. I felt for him goodness and love (not the romantic kind but the love that wants the best for the other person). Before I knew what was happening, I was asking about his upcoming wedding and wishing him a heartfelt blessing—and I actually meant it.

Unbelievable!

This forgiveness thing really works.

Through my surrender the Lord was able to produce in me some of the fruit of His spirit: love, joy, peace, patience, kindness, goodness, gentleness, faithfulness, and self-control. Instead of bitterness and anger that results from unforgiveness and entitlement, I had real joy. And something else . . . I was free.

Girls, it's time for your pop quiz. Is there bitterness in your heart today? Is there someone that you need to forgive? If the answer is yes, then take time to pray and release the person so that you, too, can know freedom from bitterness.

Dear Father,

I repent of the unforgiveness in my heart toward

_____.

[name the person or group of people]

I choose to forgive _____ for

_____.

[be specific—name any offenses that come to mind]

God, I release them to You. I forgive because I, too, am a sinner and have received forgiveness.

I pray You would bless this person.

Lord, please heal my heart of any bitterness caused by the unforgiveness.

I pray this in the name of Jesus. Amen.

Girls, you know that I understand the temptation to eat the red berry of bitterness. It appears oh so yummy. But I hope you've seen how oh so deadly bitterness is to a woman's soul. When in the wilderness and hungry for relief from pain, that berry sure looks enticing. Yet resentment, anger, unforgiveness, and hatred will flat-out poison a girl. I encourage you to choose when in a wilderness season, like my friend Becky did, to surrender your pain and unmet expectations to God and let Him work out healing and forgiveness in your heart. This, my friends, is the path of freedom and life.

Bitter or Better?

"Are you bitter?" Seriously, I almost choked on my food when I heard his question. Clearly, this guy didn't get the "What Not to Ask on the First Date" memo. The question startled me. I looked at him—more than a little perplexed—and thought to myself, *First of all, how does he know?* Then I reasoned, *Who doesn't?* And then I thought, *Is he really asking me about my last relationship, right here, right now, on our first date?* Once I got over the shock of his forthrightness, I thought about his question and answered, "Am I bitter? No, I'm better."

Now that all first-date conversation etiquette was out the window, and since it was obviously no secret that I'd just walked through a torturous season, I decided to elaborate a little more on my answer. I said, "I'm a better person because of the experience, for . . .

through the pain I learned compassion,
through the doubts I learned to trust,
through the fear I learned faith,

through the rejection I saw God's amazing hand of
protection,
and through the darkness, I saw the Light."

He didn't say much after that. I suppose I was now the one guilty of TMI (too much information)—but, you know what, it was good to hear myself say these words out loud. And yes, you guessed it, there wasn't a second date. But trust me . . . I'm not bitter.

chapter 13

Oh, Be Joyful!

In this you greatly rejoice, though now for a little while
you may have had to suffer grief in all kinds of trials.
These have come so that your faith—of greater worth than gold,
which perishes even though refined by fire—may be proved genuine
and may result in praise, glory and honor when Jesus Christ is
revealed. Though you have not seen him, you love him;
and even though you do not see him now, you believe in him
and are filled with an inexpressible and glorious joy, for you are
receiving the goal of your faith, the salvation of your souls.
—1 PETER 1:6–9 (NIV)

The massive rock face that I found myself clinging to for dear life did not seem anything at all like its name. I would have described it as "menacing," "foreboding," or "fearful," not "Oh-be-joyful." It wasn't even a pretty mountain. Instead, it was a mass of ugly boulders, dark and grey, piercing the sky—very *Lord of the Rings*. Ironically, the peak our guide chose for us to climb during this wilderness adventure was given this profoundly spiritual name—"Joy." And yet, there I was, stuck and clinging to a boulder, feeling anything but joyful, only an embarrassing twenty-five feet from the summit.

I really wanted to crawl back down, to forgo the thrill of seeing the view from the summit for just a taste of the familiar—the solid, flat ground I liked to call "safety." But looking back down the mountain didn't give me the sense of security that I desired. No, craning my neck around while still tightly gripping my new best friend, I attempted to look back down the mountain for an escape route. Oh yes, I forgot to mention one important little nugget. There was no trail on this mountain—just rock, and tons of it. Looking back only intensified my fear. For in fact, I couldn't see anything. A thick cloud, milklike in appearance (not the skim kind, I tell ya), obscured my view and left me feeling paralyzed and freaking out just a tiny bit. OK, who am I kidding? I was borderline "crazy place."

Then I heard the voice: "Keep moving. Don't give up. Take one more step. Place your foot to the left. Lean your weight against the boulder and pull yourself up." It was the voice of my guide encouraging me to press on.

Backpacking with my girlfriends was supposed to be fun: sleeping outdoors, gathering firewood, finding water, building shelter. You know, going granola. Speaking of granola, I'm sure this goes without saying that I'm not what you'd call a tree-hugging nature-girl. Now, don't get me wrong. I love the outdoors. As long as my expeditions end each night with a hot shower and soft bed, I'm all good. I'm just saying—visiting nature is fine, but "becoming one with nature" is an altogether different thing.

And at this point in the journey, I am so "one with nature" it is pathetic. It would be hard to discern where the mountain ended and my body began . . . we were "close," if you know what I mean. As I huddled next to the wall, I reflected on the fact that this trip was *supposed* to be a simple learning experience about wilderness skills, and absolutely at no point was I *supposed* to be in danger. I was in the midst of this memo to self when my guide called out again, "You don't need to be afraid. Trust me. You are almost to the top."

Sure, I trusted her, but at that moment I didn't so much love the idea of proving this trust by starting to climb again. My guide continued encouraging me by explaining that I was only experiencing what wilderness experts call "perceived fear versus actual fear." The fact that my route was unknown, the boulders slippery, and my vision limited was causing the situation to *feel* more dangerous than it *actually* was. She reassured me that this was a case of perceived fear. I was actually safe. I was in a good place. I would make it to the summit.

Still clinging to my rock, I thought, *This fear seems pretty "actual" to me.* I mulled over her advice and reasoned it must be true. You see, girls, my guide *knew* the wilderness. She was experienced, knowledgeable, and well trained. The girl had skills: climbing skills, backpacking skills, nunchuk skills, survival skills. She'd lived for months on end in the wild and hiked mountains across the globe. Needless to say, I felt I could trust her.

Yet I didn't budge. I was torn. Gripping my rock, I decided to not go up and to not go down. I would just wait. Perhaps, in some miracle of miracles, a trail would materialize—kind of like on *Indiana Jones and the Last Crusade* when the bridge appears and Harrison Ford makes it safely across the chasm. Perhaps a stair with a nice handrail or a gondola would appear if I waited long enough.

Waiting.

Waiting.

Waiting.

Alas, no magical ski lift emerged to rescue me.

Honestly, at first the only thing that tempted me to continue climbing was my stinking pride. My pride really didn't want the humiliation of scooting back down the mountain on my bootie; but then again, to go forward into the cloud—into the scary unknown—was a little too much for a girl afraid of heights.

And there, on the side of that mountain, I would still be today if another voice had not spoken to my heart: "Marian, don't quit. Don't stop. Don't fear what you cannot see. Don't turn back because the way is tough. Press on. I have something for you at the summit." And girls, let me just say I knew this voice. This was the voice of Jesus, my real Wilderness Guide, calling me to overcome my fear.

I began to pray, "Lord, I know You are calling me to climb, but I'm afraid. Help me to reach this summit. Everything in me wants to go back to camp, pack my backpack, and hike back to the car, but I know You have a purpose in this journey. Help me." And then, I heard the familiar words, "Walk by faith and not by sight."

With that, I released my death grip on the boulder and took the proverbial "step of faith." And then another, and then another, until I found myself at the summit. There I learned the reason the mountain was named "Oh-be-joyful." For within minutes of arriving at the peak, the thick clouds parted, revealing the most spectacular view. The only word to describe that moment was, yes, you guessed it, *joy*. Now, with clear vision, I could see in the distance magnificent mountain peaks and valleys, clear rivers, and wildflowers—the view from the summit was breathtakingly beautiful.

I simply had no idea what glory was behind that cloud. Inhaling the sweet mountain air, I exhaled, "Oh, be joyful!"

Don't Miss the Wild

Like my personal season before it, in this wilderness journey I faced difficulties, terrifying terrain, and moments of despair and desperation, but the ascent to the summit proved my training ground—for in facing fear I found the muscles of faith.

Sometimes walking with Jesus means our vision is obscured by clouds, and at times we face obstacles that evoke such fear that we would rather forsake the journey than keep going. And yes, sometimes following Jesus means we trust His voice even when we can't see His face.

But girls, isn't that the thrill of the adventure?

During the months of heartbreak and confusion, I sensed God speaking one message to me over and over again: "Don't miss *the wild* for the wilderness." What did this mean? Finally, I figured out this meant that I should open my eyes of faith and see the powerful hand of God moving. This phrase reminded me to not lose sight of the incredible plan of God in the midst of the wilderness—even if my perspective was temporarily limited by a cloud.

Friends, in case you haven't figured this one out yet, we serve a wild God who isn't predictable and who isn't at all tame. Much like His creation, He is gloriously wild. But isn't it His untamable Godness that makes Him so glorious?

Reflecting over the heartache, disappointment, and misery of my wilderness season, I can honestly say it was all worth it. For there, I experienced the wild adventure of trusting God.

Girlfriends, I'm so grateful that God is God, and I am not. I've learned that He desires far better for me than I do for myself. I'm so thankful that God said no to my plan because He had a far greater adventure in mind. But most of all, my heart rejoices that God didn't leave me stuck in my fear and despair, clinging to a boulder on the side of a mountain. Instead, He called me to rise and move—for the summit was too good to miss.

Friends, don't miss the wild for your wilderness.

- Trust Jesus when life seems too much.
- Trust Jesus when the trail disappears.
- Trust Jesus when the clouds roll in and your view is obscured.
- Trust Jesus when fear grips your heart.
- Trust Jesus when your plan fizzles.

When a girl trusts Jesus, the real Wilderness Guide, she places her faith in One who knows His way through the wild frontier and is familiar with her sufferings. I can tell you this much: if you choose to trust Him, your life will not be boring, and it very well may not be safe, but I know for a fact that it will be a wild adventure. So, girls, my final advice, or should I say, my last skill for you is this: don't you dare miss the wild for the wilderness.

appendix:
Survival Scriptures

What's a girl to do when she finds herself in a "full-blown meltdown"? How do you walk by faith when your emotions are spiraling toward DEFCOM 10 and you can't quite seem to get it together? Take it from someone who's been there—in those moments we must focus our anxious and troubled thoughts on the truth found in God's Word. Just as the prophet Jeremiah said:

> "This I recall to my mind,
>   Therefore I have hope.
> The LORD's lovingkindnesses indeed never cease,
>   For His compassions never fail.
> They are new every morning;
>   Great is Your faithfulness" (Lam. 3:21–23 NASB).

The following are survival Scriptures that I meditated upon during my recent journey through the wild. I also include the short truth statement that I learned from each of these verses. Read these Scriptures for yourself in context and then apply them to your life. You will be amazed at the peace and joy that result from focusing your thoughts on God's Word.

There is a God, and I am not Him!
"In the beginning God created the heavens and the earth"
(Gen. 1:1).

Nothing is too difficult for my God!
"Is anything too hard for the LORD?" (Gen. 18:14 NIV).

"For nothing is impossible with God" (Luke 1:37 NIV).

What Satan intends for evil, my God will use for good.
"You meant evil against me; but God meant it for good,
in order to bring it about as it is this day, to save many
people alive" (Gen. 50:20 NKJV).

God sees my affliction, and He is aware of my suffering!
"Then the LORD said, 'I have observed the misery of My
people in Egypt, and have heard them crying out because
of their oppressors, and I know about their sufferings'"
(Exod. 3:7).

God's perfect will cannot be thwarted! I can rest
in His sovereignty.
"Then Job replied to the LORD:
'I know that You can do anything
and no plan of Yours can be thwarted'" (Job 42:1–2).

Joy is found in the presence of my God!
"I keep the LORD in mind always.
Because He is at my right hand,
I will not be shaken. . . .
You reveal the path of life to me;
in Your presence is abundant joy;
in Your right hand are eternal pleasures" (Ps. 16:8, 11).

The Lord is my strength, and He will defeat my enemies!
"The LORD is my rock,
my fortress, and my deliverer,
my God, my mountain where I seek refuge,
my shield and the horn of my salvation,
my stronghold" (Ps. 18:2).

I will fear no evil, for my God is with me!
> "Even though I walk through the valley of the shadow of
> death,
> I will fear no evil,
> for you are with me;
> your rod and your staff,
> they comfort me" (Ps. 23:4 NIV).

If I choose to worry, I am not believing God's promises.
> "Take delight in the LORD,
> and He will give you your heart's desires.
> Commit your way to the LORD;
> trust in Him, and He will act" (Ps. 37:4–5).

The nearness of my God is my good!
> My flesh and my heart may fail,
> but God is the strength of my heart,
> my portion forever. . . .
> But as for me, God's presence is my good" (Ps. 73:26, 28).

My security is in God, not in anything this world can take away.
> "His faithfulness will be a protective shield" (Ps. 91:4b).

God is good!
> "For the LORD is good, and His love is eternal;
> His faithfulness endures through all generations"
> (Ps.100:5).

My times are in His hands.
> Your eyes saw me when I was formless;
> all [my] days were written in Your book and planned
> before a single one of them began" (Ps. 139:16).

*I don't need to know the future because my God holds the
future. My job is simply to trust Him!*
> "Trust in the LORD with all your heart,
> and do not rely on your own understanding;
> think about Him in all your ways,
> and He will guide you on the right paths" (Prov. 3:5–6).

God's timing is always perfect.
> "He has made everything beautiful in its time" (Eccles.
> 3:11a NIV).

***When I am weak, my God is strong. He gives me strength
when I hope in Him.***
> "Do you not know?
>> Have you not heard?
>> The LORD is the everlasting God,
>> the Creator of the ends of the earth.
>> He will not grow tired or weary,
>> and his understanding no one can fathom.
> He gives strength to the weary
>> and increases the power of the weak.
> Even youths grow tired and weary,
>> and young men stumble and fall;
> but those who hope in the LORD
>> will renew their strength.
>> They will soar on wings like eagles;
>> they will run and not grow weary,
>> they will walk and not be faint" (Isa. 40:28–31 NIV).

I don't need to worry because my God will provide for me.
> "Don't worry about your life, what you will eat or what
> you will drink; or about your body, what you will wear.
> Isn't life more than food and the body more than cloth-
> ing? Look at the birds of the sky: they don't sow or reap
> or gather into barns, yet your heavenly Father feeds them.
> Aren't you worth more than they?" (Matt. 6:25–26).

God loves me.
> "God proves His own love for us in that while we were
> still sinners Christ died for us!" (Rom. 5:8).
> "For God so loved the world that he gave his one and only
> Son" (John 3:16a NIV).

God works all things for good!
"We know that in all things God works for the good of those who love him" (Rom. 8:28a NIV).

I must walk by faith not by sight!
"For we walk by faith, not by sight" (2 Cor. 5:7).

Jesus is before all things, and He holds all things together!
"[B]y Him all things hold together" (Col. 1:17b).

God's amazing power is working for me in Christ!
"the immeasurable greatness of His power to us who believe, according to the working of His vast strength" (Eph. 1:19).

The enemy is defeated, and Jesus is victorious!
"He put everything under His feet and appointed Him as head over everything" (Eph. 1:22).

Faith that stands firm in the wilderness pleases God.
"[W]ithout faith it is impossible to please God, for the one who draws near to Him must believe that He exists and rewards those who seek Him" (Heb. 11:6).

There is a great purpose in this trial.
"Consider it a great joy, my brothers, whenever you experience various trials, knowing that the testing of your faith produces endurance. But endurance must do its complete work, so that you may be mature and complete, lacking nothing" (James 1:2–4).

If God says no, then He has something better prepared for me.
"[E]very perfect gift is from above, coming down from the Father of lights" (James 1:17).

God cares for me.
"[C]asting all your care upon Him, because He cares about you" (1 Pet. 5:7b).

I must be on my guard against the deceptive lies of the enemy and stand firm in my faith.

"Be sober! Be on the alert! Your adversary the Devil is prowling around like a roaring lion, looking for anyone he can devour. Resist him, firm in the faith, knowing that the same sufferings are being experienced by your brothers in the world" (1 Pet. 5:8–9).

This world is not my home!

"[T]he world with its lust is passing away, but the one who does God's will remains forever" (1 John 2:17).

Jesus is coming again!

"Look! He is coming with the clouds,
    and every eye will see Him" (Rev. 1:7a).

small-group
Questions

Introduction

1. Marian describes herself as an "ugly crier." What kind of crier are you?
2. A wilderness season is a time when faith is tested. Are you currently in a wilderness, or have you been through one in the past?
3. Marian describes the elements of the "perfect storm" (rejection, unmet desire, heartbreak, loneliness, confusion) that resulted in her wilderness season. What circumstances led to your wilderness?

Chapter 1

1. Have you experienced grief as described in this chapter?
2. Which of the five stages of the grief process are you currently in? Denial, Anger, Bargaining, Depression, or Acceptance (p. 13)
3. Marian describes the tormenting questions that assaulted her faith. Can you relate to her experience?

Chapter 2

1. Everyone experiences some form of rejection. If your life were a reality TV show, which one would best fit you?
   a. *Survivor*—"The tribe has spoken."
   b. *The Bachelor*—"No rose for you."
   c. *The Apprentice*—"You're fired!"
   d. *America's Next Top Model*—"You just aren't pretty enough or thin enough . . . ."

2. In this chapter we learned how the deep wound of rejection can lead to future bad choices. Can you trace any of your regrettable decisions to a root of rejection?

3. Having read the story of Joseph, do you find any metaphoric parallels to your life? (I say metaphoric because I doubt that there are camels in your story—however, if there are, you go first!)

4. To discover the theme of this chapter fill in the blank: *What seems like* _____ *is God's* _____.

5. How is the sovereignty of God revealed through the life of Joseph? How does this truth help you to trust God in your wilderness season?

Chapter 3

1. In the beginning of chapter 3, who did Marian say that she "fell head over heels in love with"? What elements of her testimony of transformation do you relate to?

2. Marian said it "was her passionate love for Jesus that was put to the test." How is your love for God being tested?

3. Marian explained that true worship of God is when He is at the center of our hearts and lives. In this chapter, she uncovers how Satan seeks to destroy our worship through temptation. This temptation is described as a "war for our worship." How does the realization that there is war raging

for your worship help you to overcome the temptation in the wilderness?

4. Why does Satan desire to destroy our love for God?

5. Upon realizing she was in a war for her worship, Marian said, "There was no better way for me to express my love to God than by staying faithful to Him in my pain." Here she describes making the mental choice to worship and praise God in her wilderness despite the pain and confusion she felt. How can you worship God in the midst of your struggle?

Chapter 4

1. Sarah's story brings up the question that many ask in the wilderness: "why?" How can you relate to Sarah's struggle?

2. This chapter teaches a powerful truth about our perspective on pain. Sarah said, "I knew my pain had a purpose or God would not allow it. We live in a broken world that is filled with sin and suffering. God is not sadistic. Satan wanted me to believe He took pleasure in my pain. The truth is Jesus aches for me. I know God was saying to me, until healing comes, 'His grace would be sufficient for me and *His* strength would be made perfect in *my* weakness.'" Discuss her realization. How does remembering that God is not sadistic and that He hurts for you bring comfort to your heart?

3. Sarah is a woman who has chosen to use her suffering as a means to glorify God. How can you turn your situation into an opportunity for praise?

Chapter 5

1. In this chapter Marian describes "that box" that inflicts pain. What is your box?

2. *Despair* is defined as a state of being without _____. (p. 83)

3. Have you ever been at the point where you were ready to give up hope?

4. Hagar encountered God in the wilderness when she was at a point of desperation. What did you learn about God and about the wilderness from her experience?

5. Do you ever feel "invisible" or like no one understands your pain? So did Hagar until her encounter with "The God Who Sees." Does this fact about God's character comfort you? Does it give you a newfound hope?

6. On page 91 Marian describes how the wilderness took her prayer life to a whole new level of intimacy with God. Are you real and raw with God about your pain?

   Fill in the blanks of this powerful verse of Scripture: "The righteous _____ out, and the LORD _____, and delivers them from all their _____. The LORD is _____ the _____. He saves those _____ in spirit" (Ps. 34:17–18).

Chapter 6

1. Have you ever needed God *just* to breathe?

2. What do you learn about God from Psalm 27:13–14?

3. How did this assurance give Cristy the strength to begin to climb up out of her despair?

4. How is our "hope" for the future rooted in our "faith" in God?

Chapter 7

1. Are you living with an unmet desire? What are you waiting for?

2. Women face three dangers in the wilderness of unmet desire: envy, manipulation, and worry. Which of these is your greatest struggle?

3. Marian described the danger of the "pity party" and how Satan uses this tool to damage our faith. What did she learn that helped her overcome this temptation?

4. Have you ever seen your unmet desire be gloriously met . . . for someone else? Has envy ever robbed you of the joy of sharing in someone else's celebration? Take a moment here to pause and pray for God's protection from envy and comparison. In this moment thank God for the blessings in *your* life.

5. Marian talks about "finding an alternate route" to bypass the wait. Have you ever tried to "reroute" and manipulate your circumstances? How did that alternate route work for you? What consequences did you face for not waiting upon God?

6. Psalm 37:3–7 teaches us that the solution to worry is to "rest in the Lord and wait patiently for Him." This psalm also teaches us that the way to do this is to "commit" (hand over) unmet desires to Him. What desires do you need to "commit to God"?

Chapter 8

1. How did the instructions on the "little yellow flyer" prepare Marian and her friend for their surprise encounter?

2. God's Word, the Bible, is our "instruction manual" for surviving the wilderness seasons of life. What do the following Scriptures teach you?
    Psalm 119:105
    Psalm 1:1–3
    Deuteronomy 8:1–3
    Proverbs 3:5–6
    Psalm 23:1–3
    Psalm 27:1–3

Chapter 9

1. Chapter 9 lists the warning signs of "spiritual dehydration" (p. 146). Which ones have you experienced or are you experiencing?
2. Marian says, "Desperation for [Jesus] causes a dependency on Him." How has your wilderness season revealed your desperation for Him? Are you finding yourself closer to God because of your wilderness experience?
3. Read John 7:37–39 and Psalm 63:1–5. Are you drinking daily from the "living water"?
4. Review the skills taught in this chapter for spending time with Jesus through prayer and Bible reading. Just as life without water is doomed for dehydration, a day without drinking from the Living Water is headed for trouble as well. What is your plan of action to make your daily quiet time the priority of your day?

Chapter 10

1. How did God describe Himself to Moses in Exodus 13:18–23?
2. Prior to reading this description, was your image of God's character similar or different?
3. The wilderness season can expose our deep-rooted beliefs about who God is. Has your heart believed lies about God's character and therefore prevented you from trusting Him and running to Him for shelter?
4. How did saying and calling on the name of Jesus bring peace to Marian and her friend when their emotions were spiraling into a full-blown meltdown?

Chapter 11

1. In this chapter we learned about the interaction between Jesus and Satan in the wilderness. How did Jesus stand against the lies and deceptions of the Enemy?
2. Marian gave an example from her life of how to detect a lie (hint: fake designer denim). What was the secret to recognizing a fraud?
3. What specific lies about yourself, your situation, or God has the Enemy whispered in your ear? List three.
4. Find three truths from God's Word that dispel the three lies that you have listed above. Speak the verses out loud just as Jesus did. Remind yourself of God's truth every day.

Chapter 12

1. Why is the "red berry" of bitterness so dangerous?
2. Are there any wounds in your life that still need the healing touch of God? If so, take time today to pray through the pain and ask God to begin the process of healing your heart.
3. How can unmet expectations cause bitterness? What is the solution found in this chapter?
4. Unforgiveness is one of the key causes of bitterness in a woman's heart. Is there anyone you need to forgive? If so, follow the suggested prayer on page 189.

Chapter 13

1. Marian's mountain-climbing experience paralleled the fear she felt while in her spiritual wilderness. How has fear gripped your heart in your wilderness season?
2. Fear is conquered by faith. In what area is God calling you to trust Him?

3. The final skill is "Don't miss the Wild for your Wilderness." What do you think this means?
4. Read James 1:2–4 and 1 Peter 1:6–9. What is the reason for joy in the wilderness?

Notes

1. Ken Gire, *The North Face of God* (Colorado Springs: Tyndale House, 2006), 119.

2. *Worship: That Thing You Do*, DVD, Louie Giglio.

3. Ibid.

4. Phillip Yancey, *Disappointment with God* (Grand Rapids: Zondervan, 1992), 183.

5. James Dobson, *When God Doesn't Make Sense* (Carol Stream, IL: Tyndale House, 1997).

6. Yancey, *Disappointment with God,* 183.

7. Ibid.

8. "Blessed Be Your Name," *Songs of Matt Redman,* vol. 1 (Brentwood, TN: Music Services).

9. Hannah Hurnard, *Hinds' Feet on High Places* (Wheaton, IL: Tyndale House, 1975), 172–73.

10. Buck Tilton M.S., *How to Die in the Outdoors* (Merrillville, IN: ICS Books, 1995), 16.

11. Ibid.

12. John Piper, "Rivers from the Heart" (sermon, Bethlehem Baptist Church, July 19, 1981), www.desiringgod.org.

13. *The Passion of the Christ*, DVD, directed by Mel Gibson (Newmarket Films, 2004).

14. *Dictionary.com Unabridged (v 1.1)*, s.v. "bitter," http://dictionary.reference.com/browse/bitter (accessed: October 23, 2007).

About the Author

Have you ever seen a street after a parade? The lonesome scraps and fragments that are left seem dirty, abandoned, and trashed. Run over.

What a shift from the moment before when music trilled, drums beat, people danced, and colors burst through our senses, drawing us closer and closer, the goal to press as closely to the barricade as humanly possible. What fun! What exhilaration! What glitter! What a draw! And then . . . it's gone. Passed. Done. Confetti becomes litter, songs trail to silence, and the attraction of the crowd dwindles and dies. This is how Marian Jordan describes her life without Jesus Christ.

Fun, loud, colorful, cyclical . . . lonely and trashed.

Her sharp observation of the party years resonate with the familiar. Her transparent account of the lure of fashion, sex, booze, and approval chronicle the dilemma of the "every girl" in today's society.

Marian's powerful testimony of coming to brokenness and emptiness and her dynamic account of the gentle mercy and forceful grace of Christ, who called her into His arms, permeate all of her writings and speaking engagements. Whole in Christ and ready to tell any ear that will listen, Marian has a passion for young women who flock to the parade of emptiness.

She is a dynamic speaker who leaves indelible marks on her audience: painful rib cages from laughter and mind-searing impressions of being so-dead-on to one's private dilemmas. Marian has the gift of applying sound biblical truth to the tender wounds of bleeding hearts. The girl can teach. The girl can relate. And the girl can move a wounded heart to change, through an introduction to Jesus Christ, the Lord and Lover of her soul.

Today Marian is the founder of Redeemed Girl Ministries. She is an active speaker, guest lecturer, and published author. Marian earned her master's degree from Southwestern Seminary. She lives in Houston and serves at her home church, Second Baptist Church, when not on the road at speaking engagements. Though she is a Texas girl at heart, she feels at home in destinations all over the world: Australia, Costa Rica, Italy, England, Lufkin, New York, Magnolia. She finds God's beauty in every country, city, and small town that she happens upon. So now, when she does come across a parade, she can soak in the excitement and walk away content, knowing that the Master of Ceremonies will go with her to the next town, the next country, the next season of life. And that, friends, is the beauty of being a Redeemed Girl.

If you are interested in Marian Jordan
speaking at your conference or event, contact
www.redeemedgirl.org.